About the Author

Anthony Labson is a writer who found his passion at an early age writing poetry and short stories. Finding an escape from the outside world by creating one of his own became his greatest gift. In a time where everything is remade or rebooted, he also believes creativity is at an all-time low. Now he has stepped up to bring creativity back to the world that's just sticking to used up ideas and remakes that are doomed to fail. People want something original and he's one of the people who can give you what you want.

Anthony Labson began his writing career attending Nova Southeastern University with The Knight Newspaper as a freelance film critic and writer. He's also been published in the NSU magazine, Digressions, and has worked for the magazine until graduating in 2008. After graduating, he frequently self-published poetry and prose on networks to gain momentum from readers. In December of 2011, he realized that he had more to offer, so he is taking the next step to being a recognized author. He is currently self-publishing his works hoping to gain attention from readers everywhere and become a successful writer.

The people want to see something fresh and new, not new versions of old ideas. The future is for those who take the road less traveled and risk who they are for what they can become. If you want something that's going to grab the reader's attention, then contact Anthony Labson or enjoy one of his pieces available online and in print. Actions do speak louder than words, but words always make the biggest impact. Until the next is written.

Introduction

This is a book of poetry that I wrote during the recession based on events in my life and my family and friends, as well as others I've met. The rest are poems written from the imagination. They meant to make you laugh, cry, or think. The recession changed the lives of countless Americans in different ways. Some were challenged financially and others personally, but all were challenged mentally. Uncertainty grew in the nation as planned futures were altered by the fall of the economy.

When people needed money to get back on their feet and jobs were nowhere to be found, people developed a sense of hopelessness -- myself included. But while the ones who could afford it were safe, others choose to grab whatever they could just to pay the bills. During those years I met some very interesting people -- good people who I still stay in contact with. They are people who turned their lives around from lives a crime, people who owned businesses, and unfortunately people who lost their way. How some of them stayed in good places in dark times is for them to say, but my release from the pain of reality was in writing.

Writing has always been an escape for me because of the sense that I had absolute control over what was being done. While attending college, I found my strength in poetry. Imagination in my opinion is the greatest gift we can have when reality is not a friend and there is no sanctuary to be found. Having a healthy imagination also makes you quite the dreamer. And if you're touched by one or more of the poems in this novel, one of my dreams might actually become a reality.

I will be a successful author and for that I give my eternal thanks to you. I would like to say thank you as well to Stephanie Fleming for doing an awesome job as my editor and to the employees at Glamour Shots in the Sawgrass Mills Mall, for their professional work with my cover photo. Also, thanks to my friend Ralph J. Bizzarro for inspiring me to return to writing, you're a true friend.

Text Copyright in 2012 © by Anthony Labson

ISBN-13: 978-1495967870

ISBN-10: 1495967875

Poetry about my Life and the ones who've helped me.

Personal Belief

We are all just pieces on a chess board. But we do have the power to become Kings and Queens. We don't have to be the pawns.

My Closet

Like the phantom of the opera,
I was a misunderstood monster.
Not scarred in the face by fire
but with a body of excess fat.

The demons kept hurting my soul.
They tortured me with insults.
Boys threw stuff at me.
Girls called me a freak.

I fought back with hatred and fists.
Boys lost teeth and girls lost hair.
My life was becoming a sad fable.
Dante would run in fear of my inferno.

So, I ran into my closet and dreamed
in such a small hot space.
I lived in a new world with sunlight and cool breezes.
But the breeze was just hanging clothes running across my face.

Silence.
That was my greatest ally to focus on my dreams.
There was nobody else that could distract me
when I was in that closet.

The price for paradise was cheap --
my heart and my sanity.
I had no use for those things anyway.

I wasn't happy when I had them.

Time went by fast when I was in the closet
and slow when I was out.
For 6 long hours I'd be in hell.
I would cut off my right arm
to hear that final ring.

For years I was in my closet,
praying to God for mercy.
Finally my parents found me
and dragged me out of my closet.

My parents were scared
to see their baby boy look so cold.
They couldn't understand this boy who is so sweet
look so morose and so angry.
I would try to get back in my closet,
But they would keep me out,
kicking and swinging.

Later, I was sent to see someone.
I felt like a wounded animal backed into a corner --
scared, confused, and ready to fight to the death.
The doctor looked at me with such pity.

I would say, "Go to hell.
How could you blame me for what I've done?
If you'd lived my life you would understand.
For some people, dreams are better than reality."

I met others who had my problem,

who had scars of their own
and were outcasts of society for different reasons.
Some cut their arms, some were loved too much by their parents.
There was even one boy who wanted to be 6 feet under.

Even though they opened their arms to me,
I pushed them away.
My anger made me numb from the heart down.
I was the boy with a permanent frown.

But something happened one night.
Somebody got their wish.
That boy was going 6 feet under
because he purposely drowned in his toilet.

When I saw him covered in sheets,
I realized where my anger was going to take me.
So, I decided that it was time for me to go home.
I told the doctor everything he wanted to know.
I met the requirements and became healthy again.

After months of treatment,
I was allowed to live again.
I moved away from my demons and my torture.
I now have a new home and a new closet.

But I don't use it.
I put all my clothes in drawers
and boxes in the garage.
Now, I feel the warmth of a real sun
and the smooth breeze on my face.

I still have my anger,
but I keep it under control.
I have friends now and a girlfriend.
Will it last? I really don't know.

But when I wake up in the morning
and I look at my life today,
I can actually see that my prayer was answered.
I am free from my torment and my closet.
I have been granted my mercy.

Best Friend

Our families were friends before you and I
came into this world
and their friendship passed onto us.
You were, hands down, my best friend.

You were always the athlete,
the show stopper who stood out.
You were the one people wanted to be around.
But the one person you wanted around you
was me.

I was your polar opposite.
I kept to myself. I wasn't a fan of society.
I liked to be respected for my mind
and not for my strength and size.
For that, people believed me to be disturbed.
But through the years you stood up for me.

Even when I didn't want your charity.
I preferred to stay in a closet and drift into
a false reality. But when you found out,
you helped me come into the light.

You helped me by reminding me of our youth.

When we played baseball in the street,

when you told me to swim in our plastic pool,
when we put our pennies together to buy our own pizza,
when we snuck in to see our first R-rated movie
and I'm still scared of Freddy to this day.

Playing football in the mud was the best of times,
but not as fun as actually going to the games ourselves.
We always had a blast when we went places together
and attended live events.
Football games, baseball games, and wrestling --
cheering for Mr. 316.

You saved me by reminding me of these times because
those were the best moments of my life
when I was a child because I was around you.
Deep down, you were the brother I never had.

I thought we could have moments like these again,
but it wasn't meant to be. Life was moving
and so were we but in different directions.
So, it was important to you that you leave me a
parting gift, my sanity.

You didn't want to remember me as
a sick little kid wasting his life in a dark room.
You wanted to remember me as the kid you
sat next to in class who you cheated off of, who you
purposely went to detention with to keep company,
who you hung out with every second of every day.
You saved me. So, now I return the favor in the

only way I know how to do best.

We all only meet a few true friends in our lives
and I was fortunate to have one so early in life.
You know who you are, and I want you to know
you set the bar very high for who I would consider a friend.
Thank you for saving me.

I only hope my son or daughter will be as fortunate as I was
to have a best friend when they reach our age.

Storm

I can't believe it's done.
With the touch of a needle,
my best friend is gone.
Somehow, that same needle punctured
my heart.

I got you when you were a pup.
And for 13 years, I saw you grow
into a beautiful pure black Labrador.
The kind you would see in a show.

There were great times,
like running alongside you early in the morning,
throwing the ball around the yard,
showing you off to everyone and bragging,
playing tug of war with the rope.

But there were bad times,
like you barking in the middle of the night.
Your barks would sound like thunder.
Not to mention the hours of life used
picking up after you went inside the house.

But this moment is the worst.
When I realized that your time was coming,
I knew what I had to do, but I didn't like it.
But I loved you too much
to see you suffer.

I hope I did some good in staying with you
in that silent, ice-cold room
and talking to you so you wouldn't hear
that silence till the end.

Oh, how I cried when I looked into your eyes
and told you "I'll be seeing you again."
I wonder if you knew what was coming.
Either way, I hope you knew my heart broke
for the first time that day.

I lost my first best friend.
His name was Storm.
And he was the best dog in the world
hands down.

Athletics?

Why go into athletics?
Oh, let's see -- there's
money, cars, women, millions of fans
admiring and worshipping you.
Oh, let's not forget the women.

Tons of success and
casual sex with more
women than trophies
I have in my display cases
in my million dollar house.

What more can I ask for?
It only takes a
small sacrifice.
I'll just be spending more days
on the road with a bunch of sweaty players,
sleeping more in hotels than in my own bedroom.

Then there is also the hours of practice
in the hot and humid sun with no clouds.
Let's not forget playing in the rain
to only increase my chance of injury.
Oh, there is no greater rush
then going to the hospital with a broken leg.

Flying around the country and
getting mauled and heckled

by fans of the local teams.
Trying not to lose our temper
and tear off their drunk heads,
even after they spit in our face.

Keeping an eye on my behavior,
even on my days off
because the media loves to find more
dirt on heroes than anybody else.
You can't turn your back on them.
You can't even turn your back on your wife.

Marrying a faithful woman when you're an athlete
is like choosing which knife is more likely
to break in half after hitting a part of your body.
The world has too many gold diggers.
Sometimes I wonder if I have a wife
or just a really expensive hooker.

She definitely won't be there for me
when I'm in agonizing pain.
All I'll have is the thousands of dollars
in pain killers and other medications
that I'll need even after I retire
and can't stop my hands from shaking.

No, thank you.
I'll stick to poetry.

I Have a Dad

I have a Dad.
He loves me when I'm good.
He punishes me when I'm bad.
He never does it because he can.

I have a Dad.
He loves to make me laugh because of how I smile,
no matter how lonely or sad I am.
I'm proud to be his son.

I have a Dad.
He is there to guide me,
even when I get mad
and I lose all my sanity.

I have a Dad.
He is there for my mother, sisters and me.
He always gives an ear and a shoulder to our problems.
When my other friends see us, they begin to cry.

They cry for something they don't have.
I cry because I have a Dad.

Three Mothers and A Little Tony

Whenever my mother left the house,
I was stuck with two sisters who would
act like they were the mother.
At first, I thought it would
lead me to the mental hospital.

But to my surprise,
they took care of me
and let me do what I wanted.
They never did me wrong,
even when they knew they could get away with it.

When our mother was gone and father
was at work, we were all alone.
You would open the pen and let me out.
That led to a lot of fun memories as
time moved forward and we all grew.
I loved how we
played solitaire on the computer together,
watched TV, or put our pennies together
from our jars

so we could order our own pizza.
You two were truly a blessing.

The Eldest.
The head of this group.
Strong willed, passionate, driven,
and always walking toward
a planned path. But always took time
to show compassion to a lost child
and knew how to make me laugh.
I now enjoy returning the favor and
making her laugh.

The Youngest.
The reason of the group.
Always in a book, always knew how
to speak on certain issues, head full of ideas.
How she would always read those stories
to me, filling my head with ideas.
How I hope to have her read my stories
and share them with her children.

I was not always the best brother to have
and when I wasn't, they stood by me.
They never showed me resentment
or turned a deaf ear to my pleas for help.

They have always treated me like
the little brother they let out of the pen
when mom was away and
I love them for it.

Thank you for not giving up on me.
Love your baby brother.

Two Jets and A Cowboy

Kin -- not directly brothers, but blood
could not make us any closer.
To have such bonds are rare in
this day and age where family
is a rare fortune.

With love to my sisters,
they are the best I can have,
but just as there are some things you
can tell your father but not your mother,
there are some things that you can't tell
your sisters. But I had no brothers.

But, when I finally met these two Jets fans
that were related to me, I realized
God had thrown me a curveball.
Every time we get together it's nothing
but good times under a New York sky.

The best times are always around football times,
especially when our teams go one on one.
It's like the civil war between north and south,
only nobody gets killed, of course.

Thank god we are here in this time
because having you guys in my life
in a way saved my sanity.
Any guy who is the younger brother
and has older sisters will understand.

I wouldn't sell these guys out to save my life,
but if the Cowboys ever play the Jets in the Super Bowl --
you're going down!

Another Page

I always remember
how I fell asleep in History.
I'd close my eyes in utter
ignorance
and pray for the bell to ring.

Pearl Harbor -- big deal.
They killed our men,
sunk our ships,
and brought the war to us.

Big mistake, Mr. Miyagi.
We dropped the bomb,
destroyed their cities,
and made them tap out.

It was 60 years ago.
I thought it was time to let it
go.
It was just another page in
history.
So, I fell asleep like an ass.

Now, I stand here at the
ground
that buried 3,000 people, and I
cry because while they were
being crushed and burnt,

I was laughing and eating
lunch with my friends.

I cry because I regret my
ignorance.
I feel now what others felt
the day those ships sank
and our men were being
drowned
or shot by plane fire.

I cry because I realize
that I won't be the last
to forget why we remember.

these events in history.

I will remember where I was.
how I found out, what I ate at
lunch,
who I was with, what kind of
day
it was, and how people
reacted.

After another 60 years,
there will be the another ass
who will lower his head
and wait for the bell
because to him
it's just another page.

Rest in Peace Nono

R.I.P., Nono.
A man of a great generation,
a husband of a lucky woman,
father to four little children,
and grandfather to numerous
children who have been benefited.
He came over a great sea during a time of chaos and anarchy
when the world seemed nothing but dark and dim with no light.
But he held strong against the winds of change and found a light,
and his family has benefited from his labor and his strong sacrifices.
He sacrificed by leaving his home, country, and way of life so that
his children will never have to see, hear, or feel the heartache he felt
when he was a small boy
being taken away from his
home by the forces of evil.
He was placed in a camp in
which only labor was what
keeps the person alive and
well, even with guns pointed
at you by men of your own
country. He faced horrors, the
likes of which he prayed we
will never see. He gave us this
gift of a greater chance at life.
My only regret is that I am
never going to meet another
like him because he is of a
different generation that wouldn't

understand. The idea of a world at war with each other, that you had to earn every cent that you got because the only one that can help you is yourself. He was a man of a great generation, and I regret that I wasn't a part of it. But I got a great consolation prize and that was carrying on his legacy that is encoded in my blood and in my heart. R.I.P

Mixed Signal

"Just because I dress slutty doesn't mean I am."
I heard that all the time growing up,
and, while I agree, I must confess I don't understand
why women get upset with men who still don't
get that mixed signal. So, I conducted an experiment.

I went to a club in one of my $500 business suits.
I put on my white-gold graduation ring,
sprayed on my most expensive cologne,
and purposely pulled out my wallet
just so people could see the size of it.

I sat by the bar and waited for someone to bite.
After about 1 a.m., I had a few, but they all left,
one reason after another.

"I live with my parents.
I drive a used car.
My wallet is filled with business cards.
I make a dollar over minimum wage."
I said to one of them,
"I never said I had money."

I finally understood why women still get upset.
It's a waste of time, it's annoying, and you seem to
run into the worse kind of people.

So why put up with it, I wondered?
Why waste the time looking the way you do
when all you really are doing is sending
the mixed signal?

I found out later that night.
at first I thought it was a game.
It's a lot more than that. If anything,
it's a riddle.

Like a riddle, you have to use your head
and really concentrate to see the answer
behind the question.
I learned that later when I met this woman
who looked as if she just came from Victoria's Secret
around 3am.

We sat, we talked, and we had drinks.
I told her no lies and exposed myself
on every level, holding nothing back.
She didn't seem to judge harshly,
though she did have some judgments.

After the bar closed, we walked along the beach
and sat in the sand while we each told a story.

In the end, she left first, leaving me her number.
She was a great teacher, she taught me
why women send this mixed signal
and why they put up with it.

Women who dress slutty may be slutty,
but, trust me when I say, there's more
to offer to those who dress slutty
but aren't.

Lady with the Golden Hair

Hair as golden as the sun
and lips as soft as pillows.
Eyes that are windows
to the gates of Heaven.

I would love to be lost
in your paradise.
I wish I could taste your cherry lips
and drink the juices within them.

Whenever she walks into a room,
the sunlight seems to dim.
When you open your mouth and sing,
you can make an opera silent.

With a simple touch of kindness,
you made a statue break out of his shell.
His blood raced through his veins again,
and his eyes filled with salty tears
at the sight of your smile.

I live today because of you then.
I go on now with the thought of seeing you again.
To hear your sweet voice call my name
and send chills through my body.

To feel the embrace
that can only be described as love.

Till I see you again,
my lady with the golden hair.
Love, Your Statue

Venti

Walking in 30 degree weather,
wearing shorts and sandals
in the middle of the night,
and for what?

Venti.
His height reaches my ankle
and he's a breed between a regular dog
and a farm animal.

But, unfortunately, is as fast as lightning.
When a door is left open,
it's a mistake waiting to happen and
that's what leads me here.

The odds of me finding this dog
in these conditions are as good as
a man with no tongue winning
a spelling bee.

So why am I doing this?
For one main reason.

I've been punched in the face,
kicked in the stomach,
survived a car crash,
broken my leg,
bruised ribs,

overcome illnesses.
No problem.

But the one thing that always hurts my heart
more than the unfaithful,
the materialistic,
and the dependent,

is the sight of seeing my sister's face in a pillow,
soaking the sheets in her tears
and filling the room with her sorrow
because I failed her.
I'd rather freeze to death.

Honest Word

I've never done any illegal drugs.
I've been tempted many times
by friends, strangers, even lovers,
but my answer has always been
no.

People always have asked why
and here's my answer.

My father never told me I wouldn't be anything
if I did drugs because he knew better. I knew
his idols were Jimmy Hendrix and John Belushi,
so he gave me the respect not to go there.

He didn't say it wouldn't make me popular in school
because the sad but honest truth is
some kids are popular because they can get
their hands on such items.

He just said this because it
was simple and true.

"Anthony, doing drugs is illegal and you
could go to jail for a very long time
just for being high for a couple of minutes.

And when you get out, you will wish they kept
you inside because I'll be waiting outside
to whip your ass for wasting your life."

My father is and always has been an honest man,
true to his word.
So, I gave him my word,
and I've kept it ever since.

My Savings

I'm tired of this bullshit!
It's a never ending cycle
because no matter how much I save
something always happens that
makes me waste my savings.

Tires go bad,
I go to the hospital,
computer needs repair,
phone needs repair,
hair needs to be cut,
toenails are ingrown,
loans have to be paid,
taxes go up,
gas goes up,
flu shots,
physicals,
birthdays,
anniversaries,
my girlfriend's birthday,
car battery died,
cable bills,
oil changes,
health insurance,
life insurance,
dental plan,
did I eat today?

How will I ever save money?
I'll never know.
I feel like a horse
in medieval times.
I haul shit for miles
only to get a couple of sips
at each end of the trip.

What's the point of trying to save money?
Just because you have it in case shit happens
doesn't mean you actually want shit to happen.

I'm going to go out to a bar
where guys go to see skanky girls
and shove 151 right down my throat.

At least this way,
I'll feel that I've accomplished something
that I've wanted to do for a while
with my savings.

Betrayal

Cuts, bruises and burns.
Infections from the cuts
and sore muscles when I
get hit and the third degree burns.

Hours of my life drained
and years of effort in vein
spent being loyal and taking care
of your product.

I believed in your mission
and upheld your polices.
What have I received in exchange?
Minimum wage.

Seeing others promoted over me,
time and time again, even ones I've trained.
Not one of them put in the effort that I have
or has the experience I possess, except for kissing the
bosses ass
which is where I believe they were more advanced than I
was.

If I wasn't afraid of jail
and spending the rest of my life in a cage,
I'd take the biggest blunt object I could find and
well…I leave that to your imagination.

But no, unfortunately, I live in a
"civilized" society. So, you're lucky in that.
All I can do is put my emotions in this dead
piece-of-used-to-be-wood and bury it in this book.

Farewell Address

After working for this company for 5 years,
I am done.
I'm calling it quits
and throwing in the towel.

After all the insults from customers
who didn't get their way and cried
while lying through their teeth about how they
were treated to the manager,
trying to get me in trouble just for doing my job.
So sad how I can't tell the difference between you
and the children at the daycare center.

To the kids that came over every Friday night
because your parents didn't want you around
and your only amusement was making my night
a living hell by trying to sneak into R rated movies
and then yell at me because you think I can't touch you.
Enjoy life when you occupy my job.

Finally, to the boss.
I tried for 5 long years for your approval,
to show that I could be a major player in this business.

But you were always more concerned with seeing
how many times you could cheat on your wife
with the young girls always looking for a job.

I never wanted or intended to possess such anger
but there is just so much a person can take.
So, since I can't lay a hand on you and I'm not
willing to go to jail over trash,
I will just move on and live my dream.

I won't wish anything bad for you
Because, honestly, your life isn't that good
and I know it won't get any better for you.
I'm sure if you conduct your personal life
the way you conduct your professional one,
you will have a wife that doesn't love you and
kids who renounce you as a father.

And after I leave this company today, I will dedicate my life
to making a living that will make your annual salary
make you look like the neighborhood paperboy.
This is my farewell address.
Enjoy reading it as I have writing it.

In a way, I thank you for giving me the inspiration.
A person doesn't know their value until they
have hit rock bottom and I have.
I know that I may not be destined for greatness,
but I am destined to be better than you.
Tomorrow I begin my destiny.

Clothes and Coals

One thing I always despised was
when I woke up and saw under that tree
those damn boxes on Christmas day. Tell me
where on my Christmas List did I write that
I wanted a pair of jeans, socks, and shirts?

I wanted the gun to go with Duck hunt.
Instead, I got a blue and white sweatshirt that
my mom got. What am I supposed
to do with this? And am I the only one that
was embarrassed whenever I'd find a pair
of underwear that I would never wear
in a lifetime. I could hang myself with
all the tight whites.

I wanted my video games.
I wanted my board games, my action figures and marbles
. Instead I got stuff that I would only
stuff into a closet and never see again.

I'd rather just have a lump of coal.
That way, I could throw it at something
and have some sort of fun, or maybe even
retribution. I could throw it at someone, like a
a bully who thinks he's better than me and
believes he can pick on me when he can.

Maybe a teacher who gave me a bad grade
or maybe a neighbor who gave me a hard
time. That's better than any pair of shirts.
I hated getting clothes on Christmas day.
Now that I'm older and don't have time
for my games. I just need clothes.

Submission or Pride? I Can't Decide

Children can be so cruel to one another,
and I became a victim of that cruelty first hand.
I wondered why it was considered not ok to pick on someone
based on race, religion or gender but it was ok
to pick on somebody because of weight.

Years of pity soon turned into periods of
rage, hatred, and even violence.
Jokes that would take a lifetime to tell and
words that will forever taint my soul.
So, I left a few scars of my own.
The only difference is that mine would show.

Cowards are strong with tongues, not fists.
That's when the picking stopped.
When the voices knew I would cross the line
and take things where they were too scared to go.
I found strength in their weakness and in their resentment.
I found joy once the picking stopped after years of trying to break
iron skin with hollow words responsible for the transformation.

Later, for my soul's sake, I lowered my guard but never
gave in to the resentment that follows me to this day.
But now things have changed.

When I was younger,
if someone had told me that I would die
in 12 months if I didn't lose the weight,
I would have said give me 11 months and
3 weeks
to think about it.

But now I am older and
I have friends who truly care about me
who want to see my outside match my inside.
Is that why I started? No.

My job requires lots of physical activity
that I can't keep up with because of my
lack of physical ability.
Is this why I've started? No.
Physical attraction sure sounds like enough
of a motive but is that why...
I'll save time by answering hell no!
Any woman that would just be with me
cause of the six pack can take six steps
back.

I look at my two cousins
who I've seen grow into two beautiful girls, and
I want to be alive to see them grow,
graduate and get married. Then
I also look at my nephew who was just born.
I want to be a part of his life and see him grow,
maybe into a football star, or just see him
become a great man like his father or

maybe his loving uncle.
Is this why I've started? Mostly.

It's the little part which I'm not sure about.
As I lose weight, I start to think back about those times
and all the anger comes back.
This is supposed to make me feel better about myself
and fill my soul with pride, but sometimes it feels like
submission to those words that have tainted me
like a scarlet letter.

I do notice the difference,
and I feel a new source of energy.
But feelings still remain.
I've always taken pride in myself
and my abilities because that's the way
I was brought up.

But am I feeling pride in what I'm doing,
or am I submitting to those voices?
I just can't figure out which one.

Her Boyfriend, My Enemy

She comes over to my house
with clothes soaked in tears,
marks on her face and in her heart.
They're from her boyfriend.
Now, she has come to me for help.

I tell her to leave him,
and come back to me.
"Why did we ever break up?
Why did you trade a prince charming
for a treacherous rattlesnake?

How much of his poison flows in your veins?
How bad does it blind your judgment?
If this is your idea of love,
I think you don't have a clue."

She says, "We are different people.
This isn't a west side story.
He is what I want in life.
In fact, we are going to be married.

I love you like a big brother."
That pisses me off.
I love her, but she wants him.
But I'd rather have her as a friend

than nothing at all.

I am the one she comes to when she's in trouble.
I am the one that always has her back.
"Big Brother" has to take care of business.
I tell her to stay here, that
I am going to talk to him.

She says, "No. I know what you mean by that."
I say, "I won't lay a finger on him. Just talk."
I leave my house with her in it.
She goes to my room and sleeps.

I said I wouldn't lay a finger.
I never said anything about a knuckle.

Later on that night, I go to his house
and I bang on the door
like my hand was hammer.
I yell out his name
like I was an angry father.

He swings the door open,
looks straight at me in the eyes
and shouts at me like he knows me.
But he clearly doesn't.

As he looks at my focused face,
I raise my knees between his legs.
He falls to the ground like a heavy sack
and I drag him out to the front lawn.

While moaning on the dirt, he says,
"I didn't mean to hit her.
She had it coming."
I kick him in his ribs and tell him to listen.

"I love her. I care about her.
I want to be with her.
But she loves you
and wants to be with you.
So, I love her enough to respect that.

You are her boyfriend,
but you are my enemy
and I will be waiting for an excuse
to take you out of the picture.
This is how everything will go.

Whenever we get together,
I will shake your hand,
And treat you like a brother
as long as she's happy.
And I will not touch you.
But I will give you this one warning.

For every scratch, you get a cut.
For every cut, you get a scar.
For every bruise, you get a flesh wound.
For every drop of blood, you lose a pint.

And if you ever break a bone in her body,
you'll feel pain so bad.
I will make demons in hell

lower their heads in shame.
He understands, and we part ways.

I go back to my place and she's gone.
She left me a note saying "Thank You."
I go to bed with bitter victory, and
she goes back to her boyfriend,
my enemy.

The One That Got Away

You call me up in tears
with a heart full of sorrow
and no courage to stand up to your fear
because now you are all alone.

Friends for the longest time,
I was always that shoulder you cried on
when you were hurt or sad. I wasn't your friend.
I was the brother you always wished you had.

But that would become our undoing
when I wanted us to be something more
and make Romeo and Juliet look like amateurs.
But you couldn't see me in that way, and so you said no.

Instead, you fell in love with the temp --
the one who had the flashy abs,
the cute smile, and a bright future that came
with a full wallet.

After high school you went with him,
leaving me alone in the cold and silence.
Years go by like days, and I move on,
living my life

And as for you, he kept you happy for a brief time
and made you feel as if you were the one.
Then reality hit and the problems began.
His life isn't turning out the way he wants.
His parent's refuse to pay his way.
He doesn't have the life he's accustomed to
and that turns the prince into the ogre.
This change causes him to take it out on you.

So, here we are, and you want things to change.
You ask me if the offer is still on the table,
and you try to find some love to reclaim.
No.

I remind her of the choice she made
and the actions that made her my past.
I tell her how sorry I am for her trouble but
there is nothing that I can do.

I tell her to leave him and find somebody new.
And I tell her if she needs help,
she needs to pick up the phone
and dial the boys in blue.

I have to move forward with my life, and,
I'm sorry, but that doesn't include you.

Marriage

I see everyone around me getting married
and everyone asks me why I'm not
on the bandwagon.
Well, here's my answer.

Marriage isn't just about finding someone to love.
I find that wherever I go.
It's not about having a family to me,
but I wouldn't turn down the thought.

It's not even about having the happy moments
which we all capture in the photographs.
In fact, marriage to me is about the complete opposite
of those photographs.

Marriage to me is about the struggle.

If we were happy all the time in marriages
then we wouldn't need to take those photos.
It's not about the trips to the white weddings,
the buying of a house together, or the family
trips to the amusement parks.

It's about your wife having all day to talk to you,
and the only time she does is when you're watching
the game or playing one online with your friends.

Makes you just want to head out and have a beer
with your friends.

It's about your husband getting on your nerves
because he keeps you up all night with his snoring,
and he still leaves the toilet seat up.
Makes you just want to put super glue on the seat
and wait for the magic to happen.
It's about your kids either going through
their rebellious phases, constant screaming
due to certain issues, doing everything you can
to make them happy and give them a
chance for a grand future.
Makes you just want some time alone.

But after all that, there's that one moment
when all those problems seem to disappear.
When you're all at the dinner table, and you
share that silent moment and look at each other
as if that was a psychological sense of satisfaction --
that you got through another day, together.

Then the husband and wife go to bed together,
confident in the days to come because no
matter how bad things get, when they wake up tomorrow,
they will be waking up next to each other.
And that makes life worth living.

That is what a marriage means to me,
and I have not met someone that I

can wake up next to yet.

Educations and Misunderstandings

People ask me
was I ever spanked, whipped with a belt,
grounded, had my toys taken away,
slapped upside the head, and even if I was hit
with a switch.
Well, here's my answer.

I had educations and misunderstandings.
Not to be confused with a parent that beats
for fun.
That's abuse.

An education always occurred when
I did something that I didn't know was wrong.
Educations are done with kindness
and are only meant to be done once.

If I had continued doing something after I had
an education, then it would have become
a misunderstanding.
Those hurt like hell,
and the affects are meant to be felt days later.

I had my shares of both educations and
misunderstandings,
and I know many do not agree with such methods.

But there's one thing I can say on this matter
and that is that the educations I have received have kept
me
on a straight path and out of a concrete cell.
For that, I thank god my parents were parents,
not friends.

Sudden Impact

Life was so simple before this.
Get up, eat, go to work, have fun,
go to bed, and do the whole thing over again.
But then I had way too much fun.

I was so scared when I finally found out.
When I heard you were coming I must have cried
and begged like a hungry dog to wish this to be a dream.
But in the end, there is no evading reality.

As time went by, I only imagined how this would turn out.
Things between her and I got better, but, in the end, what made
the only true difference in how this story would end
was you.

When you finally came, I couldn't have anticipated
what such force you brought with you.
Lighting couldn't have hit me with as much force
as you did when I saw you for the first time.

When I saw you breathe,
I lost my own.
When I heard you cry,
my heart dropped and eyes filled with tears.
When I saw you move,
I would freeze solid.
When you looked at me,
I was blinded by love.

How is it possible to have just met you,
and yet, as I see you lay there with such power,
it has changed me into more than just a man.
A man who is willing to die for you.

What have I become?
What am I to you who has brought this power?

Thank You

God created me with a special agenda,
and that was to give me to someone loving.
To me, it was mom but others Margherita.
I wish I saw her face on that one September morning.

I made you laugh. I made you cry.
And there were those times I drove you crazy.
For that, I'm sorry. But, in my defense, I am a guy,
and I've always had everything but my sanity.

You've watched me grow,
and become my own man.
I appreciated it when you would let me go
and try to figure out what I could.

I surpassed the expectation
of teachers who had no faith that I would finish.
They said I wouldn't attend high school graduation,
but I earned my Bachelors in English.

Things got rough for a while,
and I too lost faith in my future.
I was hoping I'd choke on my own bile
and just see myself freed of this torture.

But you caught me and reminded me

of who I was, what I have earned, and,
most of all, what I could be.
But I have to see it through until my fortune turns.

So, here I am now finishing something that should've been done,
And, when it is complete, there is only one thing to say to you.

Personal Belief

Actions do speak louder than words. But words always make the biggest impact no matter what the volume.

Poetry About Friends and Strangers

The Woman by the Bay

It's one thing to be left behind by someone
that you once loved more than life.
It's another to have gotten that love
after so much of your life alone.

That's the tale of the woman by the bay.
She sits on the beach with a scarred heart
and a tear dragging the ink from her eyes.
Her silence is speaking for her.

She is saying: I loved him
and I will not find another like him.
I go and sit by her, put my arm around her,
and tell her it's going to be alright.

She says how she has been alone,
and how men aren't attracted to her
as if it's a curse.
I can sympathize with her on that one.

I tell her of my curse.
That how I've learned from women,
how I know what it is that they want,
and how I know that I'm not part of that list.

She says how she will be alone again
because she is not as beautiful as the posers
on the magazines and in the movies.
Bullshit.

We are in the land of the blind,
And, while I am no king, I can say
only one true thing about this
woman by the bay

As I look at her watching the ocean,
hoping to see the dolphins,
and rubbing her feet with red sox
in the warm sand.

I see that she is one of the most
beautiful women I've ever seen.

Privileged Youth

I see a man who once had everything:
money, power, women, and respect.
He had the million dollar home
and predestined future ahead of him.

But in series of events, both
internal and external,
it slips out like sand in the palm of a hand.

I see how he stands at the corner of the street,
And, as he starts begging for money, he looks and
begins to cry as he wonders
how things can go so wrong for somebody
who has lived a privileged life?

As a child, he never wore the same pair of socks twice,
and he helped his father run the family business. But when
his parents died,
it all came crashing down upon his head.
The training he never paid attention to in school only made
things worse
as he wasted everything away for money to keep a lifestyle
alive,
a lifestyle that is only fit for a prince.

But the prince soon became a pauper

as his life was heading for trouble, and nobody was going
to save him.
Bills kept piling one after the other.
The economy was not working in his favor.
And finally, came number eleven.
The dream comes to an end.

He has nothing now, and, as I watch, I have
to admit that I'm somewhat
amazed.
Because it's not that he has no home to call his own
or that he doesn't have the life he's accustomed to
that makes him cry.

It's the simple fact
that he looks at his hands
with dirt underneath his fingernails,
and he doesn't know how to get it out.

Painful Goodbye

I stand over her as she sleeps in her eternal bed,
resting so peacefully after having a life so chaotic.
When we met in high school,
she had nothing but problems
that led her down a path of vices.

Some days, it was the "prescription pills."
Other days, it was "your insulin shot."
The rest of the days were spent at
the bottom of the bottle.
The only time she was clear-headed
was when she was with me.

The way she smiled around me,
how I could make her laugh, and help her ignore her pain.
The time we spent during lunch hour,
throwing food at each other, and walking around the school.
For some reason, I kept her away from those
"Medications."

But then, when time ran out, she went back.
Back to an ungrateful mother,
back to a pathetic excuse for a man,
back to an undesired lifestyle.
And when graduation came,
that was the beginning of the end.

The way she cried when I said goodbye.
It was like she knew she wouldn't see me again.
I looked for her in space and in the book, but
she was nowhere to be found.
Years later I found out why.

Now, here I am in remorse and regret.
I should have seen the signs.
I feel I've let you down.
I'm so sorry.

I only hope that when you passed it was peaceful,
and that peace is with you now.
I hope to see you again in a better
and more beautiful place.
Goodbye, Arianna. Love, Anthony.

Excuses

I truly feel sorry for this man.
He has enough money to take care of himself,
a decent education, and
a career that is not too demanding.
But he's all alone, and, I have to say,
he only has himself to blame.

"She's a gold digger.
She's an idiot.
She's fat.
She has a mole on her breast.
She too skinny.
She smells.
She has no ambition.
She has kids.
She's a cougar.
She's a hardcore feminist.
She's too liberal.
She's too conservative.
She's had too much surgery.
She needs surgery.
She's not a natural blonde.
She has no self-esteem.
All she cares about is my car.
She has daddy issues.
She's too successful.
She's just not the one."

I would say he is shallow, but, to be honest,

I think being shallow would be an improvement.
The problem with always getting something your way is that
you never learn one of life's hardest lessons.
You can't always get what you want, and,
since he wants the perfect woman and
won't settle for less, I'm certain of one fact.

This man will most likely die alone.

The Best Christmas Gift

I got the newest game console.
Now, I can spend hours of my life
playing with people all over the world
and dominating them with my "mad" skills.

I got this diamond necklace.
Now, I can brag to all the girls
about how my husband can afford anything I want
and make the others mad with envy.

I got the newest phone, and it comes with camera, wifi, radio,
pillbox, TV, army knife, corkscrew, and screwdriver.
Oh yeah, it can also make calls all over the world.
I can even make calls to astronauts in space.

I got my daddy back after he had been gone for so long
in a place where people didn't like him but he had to go for work.
He's not as I remember, though. He has trouble breathing sometimes.
He lost his left fingers in an accident and he got hit by a car
that sent him to the hospital for a while.

But instead of coming home, he had to finish his job.
He told me his friends helped him get through the days, but
the one thing that kept him going was the thought of
being here for Christmas with me and getting the chance
to be my daddy.

Now, he'll be here to take me to school, watch me grow up,
scare away
any boys brave enough to ask me out, and, most of all,
to always be there for me when I cry, when I laugh, and
when I go through phases in my life.
That's the best gift I will ever receive.

Help Me!

Help Me!

Before this knife enters

my accepting heart

with the help of my willing hand.

        Help Me!

        Before I take a swim

        off this bridge

        into the Hudson River

        in the climate of December.

                Help Me!

                Before I take the ultimate aspirin.

                With all the issues going on inside my head

                it can only be solved with this number 38.

            Help Me!

Before I take this last drink.

I feel numb and my eyes are nearly closed,

and only one more is needed to finish the job.

Help Me!

Before I make myself taller

with this rope around my neck.

Maybe then the world won't treat me so small.

Help Me!

Before I light this match

and drop it on my kerosene clothes.

Then I will become my very own firework.

Help Me!

This is all I have to say.

But, instead, I give you signs

just to see if you pay attention.

But, instead, you simply turn away.

Somebody please see

that I need you to

help me.

A Lonely Red Rose

I have hardly seen roses such as her.

So beautiful is this rose, yet it stands alone.

I wish only happiness for this lone rose.

She has so much to offer

but so little is taken.

Her flaming red hair

turning men's hearts to ash.

Her sultry body moving in rhythm,

drawing men into her web of seduction.

Her smile,

even in the darkest storm,

when the corners of her mouth curve up,

all I see is heavenly light.

Her determination to be independent

I admire the most of her.

Gold diggers are too numerous these days.

I wish for more like her.

Yet in the eyes of the ignorant,

she is just an object of pleasure.

I can't blame these fools for wanting such a rose.

But I can pity them for their ignorance

that will lead them to their ultimate regret.

I know this because I was once that ignorant,

and I am one with ultimate regret.

I had a rose such as this flower,

and I let her slip away.

Now, that rose is entwined with another.

So, to this lone rose, this is my message.

Don't be afraid by the thorns.

Like the rose I let go, you will find

they're not as many as they appear to be.

In time, you will find the one and the thorns will not matter.

My only wish is that the sorrow you've endeared

comes back to you ten-fold.

Disrespected Beauty

Cosmetics were created just
so women could have a chance
to look as beautiful
as this person in front of me.
But the real attraction isn't the physical.

She has a spirit as wild as a free animal
and just as dangerous when on the hunt.
Armed with a sharp mind and juggernaut drive,
she can hold her own without breaking a sweat.

Backing up any argument and never willing
to show incompetence just so a weak-minded fool
could feel better about himself.
Even though he has the money to take care of her
for life.

She can't be bought with green paper
and white pearl jewelry.
The only green and white she cares to see
is a grass background with a beautiful white wedding.

She has everything to offer a qualified man.
But can she find him? No.

The problem with having both
 beauty and brains
is arrogant men don't see the brains.

She would speak of the economy
and the laws of supply and demand,
but the only demand he would want
is her supply, and her only supply for him
would be a surplus of right slaps, free of charge.

When the topics of politics came up,
he would talk about being a donkey,
and, when she would walk away, he'd call her an elephant.
Then talk him down till he didn't have any peanuts.

When talks of the future are brought up,
the plans from her view go beyond years
but always find guys who look for what happens
at the end of the date.
The only thing that ends is their ambitions.

She has balanced ratio of body and soul,
but all they see is breast to posterior.
All she asks for is to be seen
for what she is: a woman.

Who has a point of view,
a political side, a faith, a life's
agenda, a career, and a desire to find
a man who won't be threatened by it.

My Friend, My Lover

My friend...my lover
I can remember how we met like it was
yesterday.
We were in college, but, instead of education,
I gained something more that day.
That's when my life truly began.
We kissed, and there's no
feeling in my lips to this day.

My friend...my lover
You are always there
looking over my shoulder,
wrapping your hands around my waist.
Feeling your breath on my neck gives me goose bumps,
like feeling a breeze after a hot sweaty day.

Mi amiga...mi amore
You got me speaking in tongues.
The one time I can keep it under control
is when it's touching yours.
Feeling the love exchange between us
in a single moment.

My friend...my lover
There are days we don't see eye to eye.
There are times we need our space.
But there's that moment in time when we realize
that being apart is time wasted.
Being happy without you is something
I just can't pretend.

Ym...fre...in...lmy...ver....
I can't even think straight
because my mind is full of thoughts of her.
When can we make love next?
Will she wear that for me?
I want to spend my life with her.
I want her to be the mother of my children.

You are my friend.
You are my lover.
Without you, my life would end.
Without you...I lose my purpose forever.

I Would've Rather…

I would've rather fallen off the Eiffel Tower
and landed on a white picket fence.
At least I would've seen it coming,
unlike the knife you used
to stab me in the heart.

I would've rather gone on a date with
Ted Bundy, BTK, Jeffery Dahmer, or, hell,
why not a member of the Manson Family?
At least I knew I was going to die.
Because of you
I'm dead from the heart down.

I thought I was going out with an angel of God.
But while my back was turned and my ears plugged,
you did more with complete strangers than you did
with the man that gave you everything.
You turned out to be a bitch of the devil.

I gave you everything and never
said no to anything you desired.
But when my future became insecure,
you jumped on the next luxury liner
going into your port.

At least one thing I will say.
And that's I'll have the world's biggest smile
when you meet your Brutus
and he leaves you when
you start turning old and gray.

And when you grow old and gray,
I hope you realize what you had
because when you go six feet deep,
the only friend you're going to have
is Judas.

The Heart of Dover

She came from the garden of a city,
with an appetite for something new.
She wanted a new venue and a new beginning,
and she got it clear across the country.

For a short time, she was happy with what she found.
She found friends. She found family.
And she found the beach.
She came here with her exotic ways
and made an impact in some lives, including my own.
Hair as black as a new moon night
and eyes that make you feel safe when they look at you.
It was easy for us to be drawn in by her.

But, in the end, as she felt the sand
beneath her feet, she felt like a flower in the desert --
alone and isolated.

In an area that is surrounded by water,
she, for some reason, cannot get her fill.
She missed being with the other flowers
in this part of the garden known as Dover.
Some have their hearts in the Highlands. Her heart was
there.

Not even this beach she sits on can make her smile.

She says her heart was still in the garden,
and that's why she had to leave.
She says she'll never be happy, and she is dead
without the comfort of Dover.

It's ironic because
I'll always consider her the heart of Dover.
She's the only reason I care about that location.
She's the only reason I go there.

Out of War, into the Battlefield

A solider is in a prison of my own country.
He has saved and taken lives
and drawn and spilled blood.
But that's not why he's here.

He left the war after years of service.
He went home as a hero
but was treated as a criminal.
People would gather in front of my home and shout

"Baby killer!
Murderer!
Barbarian!
Psycho!"

He thinks,
"Who are these people to shout at him?
How dare 'civilians' question a solider?
How many times have they slept on the ground?
How many times have they been under fire?

You didn't go where he did.
You didn't see the things he saw.
Your friends didn't die in your arms.
You didn't have to wait days to take a shower.

to be rid of the mud, blood, and shit on your skin.

You didn't see body parts
of all ages, of all sexes flying in the air.
You didn't see explosions happen twice a day.
And, most of all, you didn't see children cry
after they saw you kill their parents because they tried
to kill me."

He wanted to rip his eyes out
to be rid of the images that plague his mind.

Because of men like him
those horrors never made it here.
And this "civilian" has the balls to shout at me?
Where were those balls
when "his country" needed him?

But words are not why he's here.
He has heard worse than the screams of idiots.
Try going to bed constantly hearing the sounds of "real men"
scream in pain after amputations without morphine.

He's in the prison because of a small piece of fluid.
"A civilian" came up to him
and spat in his face!
That's why he's here.

The soldier thought,

"You spit on me, you spit on my platoon.
You spit on my platoon, you spit on the army.

You spit on the army,
the force that's responsible for you to be able to spit on me?"

Men like him demand respect
because, unlike civilians, soldiers have our sense of honor.
So, for that honor which the soldier prized more than his life,
he wiped the spit off his face
and slapped it back on the civilian's.

This is why he is here.
It's unbelievable that a solider would be a prisoner
of the very country he worked so hard to protect
over the rights of a "civilian."

No matter what happens to him now,
he's decided to go back to the war.
Because, unlike the battlefield here,
in the war, the enemies aren't hard to see.

The Deviant

If God forgives killers, rapists,
and all forms of evil,
why is being what I am
a one way ticket to hell?

I have a common name
you would give to any other child.
Yet you look at me like my name should be
Hitler, Bundy, or Dahmer.

If God is my judge, jury, and executioner,
if his judgment is the only one that matters,
then who the fuck are you
to tell me where I'm going when I'm gone?

To say I will burn for eternity
in a constant lake of fire.
Compared to the pain I've suffered from you,
the lake of fire sounds like a blessing.

You say my culture is evil,
yet you've never experienced my culture.
You're like a blind man,
speaking about violence in television.

Where do you get the balls
to talk trash about the way that I live?
The way you talk trash about our culture
is like how a child doesn't want to eat spinach.

Without even touching it,
you see something that looks disgusting.
Even though it can make you a strong person,
you still turn it away and you hate it
because of how it looks.

If Jesus says love your enemies as well as your friends,
then why do you harass me?
You insult me with words
and hit me with your fists.
Your souls must be dried up
because I've been surrounded by mountains of salt.

All because you don't know me.
You only know that I love something you don't.
I've done nothing wrong except being me,
And, what hurts the most is, you'll never change.

You're completely dead from head to toe.
You can make a quadriplegic feel grateful.
For that I will always pray and yet pity you
and this is the reason why.

You live by the book,
always fearful of the very word damnation.
But, in reality, you've hardly ever paid attention
to the simple meaning of life:
"To live and let live."

You judge me because you want to be God yourself.
Who the fuck are you to be telling me how to live
and how to act with my life when you're as mortal as me?

Maybe it's you that should be named Hitler.
You're being more of a heretic
than I ever could be.

You hurt me with your words
because your being so devoted.
Have you've ever listened to the word?
Deaf men look at you and think God made you
as a joke to make them feel better.

You beat me with your fists
because you're getting tired of beating your wife.
who only wishes that she could be just as happy as me.
Since she's stayed with you so long,
this shows that she has bigger balls than you.

You can't love me like other enemies
because I'm not your enemy.
I'm something you want to be:
a person.

So, I will go on ignoring you.
What happens to me when I die?
I will leave that up to God,
the creator of you and I.

A Lost Man

I met a man on the street,
and he spoke out against education.
So, I asked why?
He said,

"Because I wonder what the hell I turned my life around
for.
When I was 11, I sold crack a block away from my house,
And, by the time I was 14, I already had hundreds
of dollars hiding under my bed. I never knew
how much I had. Why?

Because my mom found the money
and turned me into the police.
Because of what she did, I got
some leniency, but I'd rather have stayed in prison.
I hated her for what she did.

While I was in the pen,
she came to visit me and told me
that I had to change my life, that
it would get better if I did
'Honest work.'

I knew that now I was on the radar.
I really had no choice.
Once I was out, I started paying attention in school
and my grades improved.

I tried going for sports,
but that wasn't working out so well.
Got a part time job working at a hardware store.
I wasn't making anything compared to what I made
selling drugs.

She tells me go to 'College,'
and things will get better in your life.
So I did. I went to community for 2,
then went to a private for another 2.
Put myself thousands of dollars in debt,
and got a Bachelor's degree.

Do I have a better life now?
No.

What do I hear from businesses?
'Sorry, we're not hiring.'
'We have no opportunities for a man of your skills.'
'You're just not the right candidate.'

Again I ask, 'What the hell did I go to College for?'
Just to have the same job I had when I was a kid,
working with idiots who have no futures
and working under a boss who went into the workforce
after high school who doesn't have a degree?

He orders me around and yet I have the degree?
This is why I turned my life around, just to be under
this dumbass's boot heel?

I was better off dealing drugs.
At least I wouldn't have the problems I have now.

But, no. For my mother, I chose to do
'Honest work.'
I see now she was naïve because, from what I see,
the way things are done around here is:

You either do 'honest work' all your life,
so someone else can enjoy the fruits of your labor
until you retire at which point you're too old and
sick to enjoy the money you earned.

Or
You do dirty work and make a lot of money
and enjoy it while you're young and can
only answer to yourself,
just as long as you can be smart about it
and stay under the radar."

I shook my head at the man and said,
"We are all on the radar, no matter how
much we try to stay under. We all also
have problems that we can't deal with. They
could be taken care of with the help of
'dirty work,' but there's one problem with that.

'Honest work' only affects our lives and nobody else's.
Your line of work destroys someone else's,
and, while I blame the individuals that say yes
to your products, I also blame you.

Because you knew what would happen
to that person and didn't care.
If you can live with that,
then that's on you. I'll be out here,
and you'll end up in prison and
die
in a concrete cell, freezing and lonely,
with nobody around to mourn you.

Thank god for 'dirty work' right?"

A Man's Girl

I see a man's girl
and I can't help but admire.
Hair that must be made of gold and
just as valuable.

Her eyes.
They burn of fire
that raises to a temperature
that can thaw the coldest heart.

After I looked into them,
I realized that Heaven exists
because I knew I was looking
at an angel.

That's when I began to know her.

How she grew up ill,
fighting a disease that keeps her down,
having her head facing down
and drowning in a sea of sorrow.

Until the day
a black knight
came and took her by the hand
and pulled her out of the sea.

Now her head never looks down.

Years have passed,
but her beauty has stayed the same.

Her body is worthy
of a sculpture's chisel,
and a spirit that needs no
holy blessings.

At first she started out as
just one of the ordinary.
But now she's turned out to be
the kind of girl every man dreams of.

Strong, Passionate, Loyal, Sensual,
Intelligent, and, most of all,
Unique.
And I'm honored to know her.

I'm a Winner

I'm here at my movie theater.
I'm the general manager.
I'm wondering why I keep going
when I can't stand my life anymore.

I have a job I never wanted,
a wife that never wanted me,
dreams that will never be reached,
and a life not worth living for.

I spend most of my time
getting yelled at by parents.
They yell because of many things
I have no control of.

The prices are too high,
they don't like how we do business,
but, the worst complaints of all,
are when they complain for their children.

They keep preaching on and on
How their kids are so
innocent and sweet.
They're little angels.

Angels have beautiful singing voices.
Their kids can make Beethoven
thank God he was deaf.
Angels are creatures of Purity.

Their kids are creatures of the Apocalypse.

They act like they know how they've been acting here.
I know how they've been acting here!
I know
cause I've been the one kicking them out.

It's always the same story.
They won't shut up or,
they won't turn off their cell phones.
But the ever popular excuse is that
they are too young to see an R-rated movie.

I've heard kids use obscene language
and seen them do unacceptable acts.
The parent's excuses are always the same
and their anger is all too familiar.

"They have my permission to see this movie.
My children deserve to see this movie.
You have no right telling my kids what they can't see."
This isn't your house you ignorant fools!

This is a place of business.
We are not a five star restaurant,
but we still have rules.
If you don't want to comply,
then get the hell out!

I'd give my right arm to say these words
to those ignorant fools.
But, instead, I have to take it

and pretend I give a rat's ass.

This is how my life is
and it will be this way
24/7 for life.
So why not end it?

Because I look at a picture on my desk
of a beautiful 2-year old girl with blue eyes.
I take all this abuse
because she won't have to.

I could just blow my brains,
but that's for people who have nothing at all.
That is only the way for true losers.
I have something very dear to my heart, and it's
the love of my little girl.

Even on the worst day of the year
when I go home frustrated, angry, and tired,
the moment I walk through the door,
she is standing there with a smile and says
the sweetest thing a father could hear.
"Daddy!"

I pick her up, and I hold her so tight.
When I look into her eyes
and see how she looks at me,
I realize something so true.

In the eyes of others,
I might be a loser.

But in the eyes of my little girl,
I'm a winner.

Who Has the Real Problem?

I walk along the beach,
an old man watching me,
thinking about all my problems.
He gives me a look
as if he were looking into my soul
with reaper-like eyes focused on me,
like he knows what's going through my head
just from the worried look on my face.

My job pays minimum wage.
I'm have debt that I will never be pay off.
I live in a neighborhood fit for a beggar.
I can't keep a relationship for more than a month.
I haven't gone out on a date in months.
I get no credit for my hard work at my job.

My parents are always complaining about how I live.
Mom complains about my diet,
that I don't call them much,
and that I don't have a life in general.

Dad complains how I don't act like a man,
that I complain too much instead of
taking care of my problems,
but he doesn't understand.

How I could deal with such problems I have?

None of my friends have the time to hang out.
I'm wondering if they even are my friends.
I can't afford to do anything fun.
I drive a car that a scooter can out run.

The old man shakes his head left and right, as I watch him as he sits
in his throne on wheels. I wonder why?

The Devilish Angel

She's the kind that is good and pure,
to be the quiet librarian or the sweet straight A student.
But it's just so much more fun to be
like a drug that kills when you overdose.

She's the kind of angel that will get on her knees
and pray for you, but, secretly,
she wants to put you on your knees
and make you bark like a dog in submission.

She lives in isolation when the day comes.
But when the moon is full and stars surround her,
she puts on a show that defines seduction and leaves
the wolves alone to howl to the moon by themselves.

She is an angel in plain sight but with evil tendencies
hidden underneath her scales covered by angelic skin.
She is a tease, a lover, an adulteress, a sinner, and a show
who will drain you of every bit of energy.

Then when every bit of your energy is spent,
she leaves you alone and flies somewhere else.
She is every bit of a devil hidden as an angel
and God help me.

I love her for it.

The Check

(Son)
Thank God I'm going to college
and getting away from you, mother.
I don't even get a congratulations
Because, now that I'm getting an education,
you're losing an income.

I don't understand why!
How could you do this to me, mom?
I am your son, and you treat me
like a kid treats an old toy.
You toss me out of your way
once I've outlived my usefulness.

When I went to school,
you never made me lunch.
I don't recall you even looking at my report card.
I don't even remembering hearing you say
"Have a good day" or "I love you."

You always didn't like to look at me anyway
Because, when I was young, you always said that
I looked like Dad and that made you angry.
Grandma told me how you used me to get Dad to stay
like a master uses fear on a slave.
All that did was give him more reason to leave.

So not only did you deny me a father,

you didn't even try to be a mother.
The only contribution you made to my life
was that you gave it to me, not because you wanted me,
because you got a free income once a month.

The only reason I'm saying this now is because
after today, a paycheck from Dad is not the only thing
that will not come to this hell hole anymore.
I'm sorry for two things Mom.
That we had to turn out this way,
and that you're not even going to say goodbye.

(Mother)
So, you think it's always been about the money?
It's so easy to think the worst of me.
You're right. I'm not going to say goodbye
because you're not going anywhere,
because you're your father's son,
and you will end up like him --
a nobody.

You won't go far in life for one simple reason.
Trash can't be anything else but trash.
You were born in this hell hole, and
you're going to come back to one,
writing a check to some girl you knocked up.

You can hate me if you want because it's not like you know
what really happened between your father and I.
If you only knew how he took advantage of me,
how your father tricked a naïve girl

by using snake-like charms and
dominant influence over me
just to get what he wanted.

He came up to me,
saying I was the one.
Then, as soon as I gave him everything,
he became a complete stranger.

He didn't talk to me for weeks,
never called to see how I was doing,
and the only time he spoke with me again
was when we found out we were having you.

The only reason I had you wasn't money.
The reason you're alive is because I am pro-life,
and when you're father found out about you,
he tried to turn me pro-choice.

(Father)
I got your letter
and thank you for letting me know
how you feel about what you've heard.
You deserve your anger, but let me help you direct it
by telling you the whole story of what happened
between your mother and me.

As far as being called
a snake and using dominant influence,
the only one that used these
in the short relationship with your mother

was in fact your mother and not I.

All I ever used was my confidence,
my reputation for being a ladies man.
Your mother would know about snakes
considering how she danced in front of me
that night in the club where we hooked up.

To say she was naïve when she was young.
Ask your mother how naïve she was
when she seduced me while the girl I was dating
was away, and I was left alone for the weekend.
I was the naïve one, thinking
I could get away with one night.

Then your mother told that girl the second she got back,
and that girl called me the same day and told me
that we were finished. So, in one night,
I ruined a great relationship because of your mother,
and I was going to be damn if I was
going to let her ruin my life.

Yes, I did try to get her to give you up,
only because she didn't want you for the right reasons,
and I didn't want you because I wasn't ready to be a dad.
I'm sorry to be cold, but you're a man and deserve the truth.
I'm not writing to justify my actions,
just explaining why those actions happened
the way they did and that I'm sorry
you got the short end of the stick.
I enclose one last check to you, so I can at least contribute to
your life.

This is more than I can say about your mother.

(Son)
After a few weeks here in college,
I've had some time to think
about all I've learned about
both sides of the whole story.

I'm writing this letter to both of you now
because I've never been so disgusted by 2 people.
Knowing both sides of your stories, I conclude
that you both deserve each other.

Dad, thank you for understanding my anger,
but to hell with your damn check.
I never wanted it. I wanted you.
I wanted a father and instead I got paper
with a cold, black, and worthless signature.

You're nothing to me but a name
because that's all I've ever seen of you,
once a month on a rectangular piece of paper.
I took that last check you sent and trashed it.

Now, as far as you go mother,
the only reason you kept me with you
was to keep Dad with you, and when that failed,
you took it out on me, and that I will not forgive.
You were more of a curse than a mother.

The only time we ever talked was when

you tried to get me to not go to college
so I can stay home with you
because you "Needed me at home."
You are just as selfish and pathetic as Dad.

And you were wrong.
I'm not like dad because I have a fiancé
and she is pregnant with my child
and we are having it together.
So, already I have out done both of you
and I conclude this letter
with these final words.

Neither one of you has contributed in my life.
You both would've done me a favor by killing me
because I hate having these feelings for you both.
Everything I have gained has been through my hard work.
For that, I doubt now more than ever that I am your offspring.
After I write this letter, I will be changing my name.

I'm attending college, I have a great job,
and I have a girlfriend who will likely be my wife.
I will have a happy life which is something you both
know nothing about. For that, I pity you.

So, I enclose to each of you
a check with my old name on it.
Treasure it because it's the last item
that will have my former name.
Goodbye.

Teachers and Cops

I walked into an argument at a restaurant the other day
between a bartender and a man who said,
"I teach 5th graders who have more common sense than you."

The bartender said,
"And I make more money in a month then you do in a year."
The teacher got angry and threw a glass on the floor
as he left in anger.

I felt sorry for him because, in a way,
the bartender was right.

Teachers.
They are the guardians of the future,
making sure the next generation is
ready to take the bar to the next level.

So how are they treated?
Like they are waste management
trying to sort out the trash from what
could be treasure.

Instead of giving them the tools

to make sure every child doesn't end up
like trash, they are given substandard equipment
that runs on ineffective policies that cripple
the victims.

Because we live in a time where budgets are the only concern
instead of making sure the victims
have a chance at a future,
the teachers are the ones who suffer greatly.

Bless them for doing what they can with nothing, but
nothing is not going to save the victims,
unless those who have the power to act finally live up
to the responsibilities they swore to uphold.

The victims don't deserve it and especially
the teachers because they are doing their job,
and, considering what they have to deal with,
they shouldn't be going on strike,
and they shouldn't be making less money
than a bartender.

                      I sat at that bar,
         after they cleaned up the broken glass,
              to enjoy some cinnamon whiskey.

                                          On the news
                 was a story about a major police department.
                         They were cutting salaries again

for the third time.

Cops.
The people we turn to when
we are in trouble and
are responsible for keeping the peace.
As much as I may disagree with some laws,
it's truly an insult to put your lives on the line
for pennies.

We may not like them when we speed.
We may not want them when there is a party.
But when there is trouble around,
we pray they're there to do
what we don't want to do,
and what they are trained to do.

It's always better to be around cops
that have nothing to do
than cops who have a lot to do.
To those cops who have a lot to do,
thank you for keeping the fight going.

When I hear about a cop taking money,
I know it's wrong and he shouldn't have done it,
But, to be honest, I actually understand.

If I was putting my life on the line every day,
the last thing I would want to make for it
would be damn near minimum wage.

But it's good we catch them,
so they don't infect the good ones.

To those who are the real deal,
that believe in the oath they took
to enforce the law even though
nobody is enforcing you're due salaries --
thank you isn't enough.

Ode to Single Parents

When I young, there was a saying
"If you were born into a wealthy family,
then you had it made."
But now it seems to be if you're born having both parents,
then you're lucky enough as is.

Marriage was seen as a sacred institution
between man and woman when they realized
that they were the ones for each other.

Now, to me, it seems like a game
to be quit and restarted
at the first sign of difficulty.
That first sign is usually
the sign of new life.

Instead of being responsible and living up
to what is owed to a true innocent,
they run like a true coward does,
and I condemn them for it.

A child runs out of fear
and whines when things don't go his way.
An adult accepts what happens
and tries to make the best out of a situation.

How can I condemn them for it?
Who am I to condemn?

I am a child of two parents who stayed together
and worked together to make sure I grew up right.
Meanwhile, over the years, I watched how
other parents called it quits.

Because of that, their children,
whom I once called friends,
became cold and isolated themselves
by going into darker places that even I
have not gone to. Some became the living dead
while others just stopped living.

That's who I am. Now, answer my question:
Who are you?
To rob a child of having a father to defend
or a mother to nurture all because
you got scared and didn't want
to own up to your responsibilities.

I don't care that you live up to your responsibilities
as a spouse or a lover.
Live up to your responsibilities as a parent.
Don't send them a check, don't send them a card,
and don't bother with a phone call.

I am a witness to a damaged generation,
and to the parents who try to fly it solo:
Thank you for showing how strong a human being

can be when pushed to such boundaries.

Personal Belief

It's not just about what you know. It's about what you're willing to do to make it in this world.

Poetry based on my Imagination

A Fallen Angel

An angel is falling from the sky.
She is in a vortex, helplessly
going down a downward spiral,
screaming for help in mid air.

She looks so pure and innocent.
She is an angel, but she can't fly.
And, as I look with a hawk's eye, I see
her wings are broken.

I wonder why she has been sent to this realm,
a realm of my vision,
an endless forest were disruption meets oblivion
and lost souls meet renaissance.

She lands in the lake of my forest.
She is 5 foot 2 and about 130 pounds,
But, like a small stone, makes no splash,
just ripples in the water.
Yet, the impact sounds like that of an atom bomb.

I get on my stallion, the eternal mustang,
and ride to the lake where I see her
floating on her back like a flower.
I pull her out and go back to my cabin in the forest.

I put her in my bedroom
because there is no other.

I sleep in front of the fireplace
and wonder where to start.

The next day, she wakes up,
and I come in with breakfast.
She is startled, but I calm her down.
I tell her that I am a friend.

"I am one who cares for all.
I give comfort and shelter to those in need.
You may simple call me friend
because that's all I'll ever be."

She eats the eggs I've made for her and
drinks the water that I've purified.
After a while, I finally ask her,
"Angel, why did you fall from the sky?"

She says, "I lost my way.
I just got bored with eternity,
so I wanted to leave.
I got my wish, and now I have nothing.

That's why I guess I'm here,
to be forgotten."
I say to her, "He doesn't forget, and he does forgive.
Somebody so beautiful should express happiness, not fear.
In time, you will learn to smile again
and never again feel sorrow."

With her wings wrapped and her body healed,
she begins to live with me here in the forest.

We take walks in the morning to see the sunrise and
have dinners in the front window of the cabin to see the sunset.

I cook her all my favorite recipes
from lasagna to baked ziti.
But when we get to the desert --
freshly made cherry pie -- her favorite.

Weeks after her arrival, she asks me,
"Why are you here?"

I tell her the truth.
"I was once lost like you were.
I fell just as you did, but found my way.
But unlike me, you still have a choice."

She asks, "What kind of choice?"
I say, "You'll know it when you feel it."
She gets confused, but, months later,
confusion turns into compassion.

Many times, she welcomed me to bed with her.
Every time I declined, not because of un-attraction.
It was just going to make it easier on me in the end
because I knew the day was approaching.

A year has passed. Her wings are healed.
She flaps them up and down
and gets herself off the floor.
I smile at her success, but she can see
my invisible frown.

The time has come, and I say, "Let's go to the lake."
But when we go, there is no lake,
just an open field with a ray of light in the middle.
She sees now the choice that must be made.

Leave or stay?
There is no turning back.
But, before she makes the choice,
she asks me with a heart-broken voice,
"Why did you stay?"

I say, "I wasn't the first.
I knew I wasn't going to be the last.
I made the choice to stay
and help other angels like you and I."

She asks, "What if I stay with you?
Help other angels by your side?
I can't image eternity alone.
I don't want that to be your fate."

I say, "That's not your choice to make.
This realm is of my vision.
This is my eternity, and this is how I choose to spend it.
If you decide to stay, I will be the one that goes.
Either way, one of us is leaving, and it's going to be you."

She says, "How do you know?"

I say, "Because you've learned again what's most important.
Eternity is what you make of it.
This is mine, and I do it with pride.

Now you can go and find something to take pride in."

Angel says, "I will miss you.
You gave me back so much."

I say, "You're welcome.
That complement is why I do this.
Now, it's time to fly."
She hugs and kisses me goodbye
then slowly moving towards the light,
never taking her eyes off me.
With new wings, she heads back to paradise.

As she disappears into the light,
I say, "Lord,
your child has returned to you.
My love and wishes go with you angel."

I turn back and head for my cabin.
My energy is now spent.
My body is weak.
My head is light as a feather.

I now go to bed and sleep
until the next is sent.

The Greatest Pleasure

After years of sleeping
in a box of metal and stone,
I'm free.
Free to indulge in pleasures.
but there is only one pleasure I want.

It's the greatest pleasure of all.

Will I get a decent hot meal?
Even though it is an upgrade
from the gruel and meatless meatloaf?
No.

Will I sleep outside under the stars?
That for me is like a blind man at an art show.
I wouldn't know the Pegasus from the Dippers.
The only thing I would appreciate is the extra space.
No.

What about making love to a beautiful woman?
To have my hands on a pair of firm breasts
and be between the smoothest thighs a woman can have.
To be squeezed by them as I dance between them.

Oh, that is indeed a great pleasure,

but not the one I speak of.
The illusions in prison quenched my thirst for lust.
This is not the pleasure I speak of.

The pleasure I speak of
is the only way I could get to a hot meal,
or sleep outside under the stars,
or find the love of a beautiful woman.

The greatest pleasure of all is this.
Now that I am released,
I will go to a motel and get a room.
Then, for the next couple of hours,

I will keep opening and closing my door.

The Gift or The Curse

Imagination.
That is arguably the greatest gift
that people have in this world.
It has helped mankind progress
by laying the ground work to a foundation.

We've dreamed of flying high into the sky
and, for generations, used various methods.
But, eventually, two brothers made history,
and now millions can touch that very sky.

We've dreamed of connecting with others
as far as continuants away.
It started out through transfers of paper,
then it evolved to party lines.
After that, mobility came, and it
even had an wristband.
Now, I can call to my friends in England
through a cell or see them on my television.

It's helped heroes become legends
and give us the motivation to follow
and surpass through various means.

We read of Hercules, and we find new ways
to achieve physical perfection.
We read of missions to the moon,
so we find ways to see the stars.
We read of people who achieved glory
in times of strife, and we find ways to lead
by their examples.

We've created civilizations
that have become an example of how
human beings should live their lives
and represent what it means to be a person.
Civilizations that have learned from the mistakes
of failures and have set up barriers to secure its
safety.

Imagination is a tool
that can be used to improve life
and secure the future for the other
generations.

However,
there is one problem with a gift.
It comes with an equal --
the curse.
The ones who would use it for
means that would only end in
self-destruction.

Our biggest threat to our future is that
it's always going to be in our nature to destroy.
Ever since we first walked, it started with clubs,
then came rocks, bows, swords, axes, poisons,
catapults, daggers, bullets, cannons, assault rifles,
semi-automatics, full-automatics, shotguns, gas,
RPGs, grenades, air-bomb, atoms, nuclear,
and the mother of all bombs.
What's next?

The civilizations we grow up
learning about and admiring their accomplishments.
They could've been spared had they not succumb
to the selfish desires of others
who lacked the imagination to see beyond their choices.

The real victims are the people who suffered from the ones
who had imaginations but for sick and depraved reasons.
The people who have talents in means of
"interrogation," or the psychopaths who are just looking
"for a good time."
This is the curse of imagination.

Both are equal in terms of
Tangibility and Motivation.
It can either be a tool or a weapon,
a gift or a curse.

And, like beauty,
it's all in the mind of the beholder.

How to say "I Love You."

Don't say "I love you"
with a serpent's tongue.
Spreading your false energy
through my veins -- that's worse than
any venom and murders the heart the quickest.

Don't say "I love you"
like a child does a toy,
something that is to be enjoyed
for a short period time and then discarded
without a care for the one who is used
and will be left alone in dark misery.

Don't say "I love you"
at all.

Give that person a gift
at an unexpected time,
and give it for no reason.

Kiss that person,
not with lustful intentions
but with meaningful ones.

Do something for that person,
not because they asked
but because you want to for them.

Be there for that person

no matter what the reason,
even when they don't want you to.

Look each other in the eyes
and enjoy that moment of silence,
that moment where words have no purpose.

Finally, hold that hand.
That is always the first step
and will always be the most important one.

If you want to say "I love you"
and actually mean it.
Then don't say it at all.

Rocks and Diamonds

I went to a garden and saw a bunch of flowers where
some had died, one was dying, and the rest were fine.
I was confused by this mixture of life and death in this one
spot of the garden covered with fresh soil over the sun.

I brought up the dead flowers with much ease,
and, to my surprise, the abuse wasn't visible on the outside,
but the root of the problem was the roots.
The roots weren't wrapped around fresh soil but rocks.

These rocks abused the roots causing the flower to
slowly die from the inside.
Instead of growing and living full lives, they absorbed
these chunks of dead weight, and it lead to their deaths.

I dug around one of the healthy ones carefully not to kill it.
What I saw was nothing short of amazing.
There was a diamond deep within the roots.
I was tempted to take it, but then I realized
what I would be taking.

These are some of the most beautiful flowers I've ever
seen.
Healthy, full of pedals, and giving off a heavenly aroma
that could paralyze someone's thinking

and make them forget all irrelevant thoughts.

So what if this diamond had something to do with it?
If this diamond is responsible, I'd be destroying something unique.
I left the diamond alone and placed it back, but then I wondered
what to do with this one flower slowly dying?

After digging around it I noticed it had been abused by some rocks,
but it was still alive.

Color was faded and down to its last pedal.
There were obvious reasons to just be rid of it, but,
if it's going to die, I'd rather it be on its own terms, not mine.
So, I dug out the rocks I found, trying not to hurt the root.
I put what soil I could, added fresh water, and waited for the sun.

Once it came, I left with saying a prayer for that flower.
Life is too short and even shorter for others.
Keep digging, precious flower and hopefully soon
your roots will wrap around a diamond,
and you will blossom into something beautiful.

The Kiss

In this moment, I am truly alive.
With blood pumping, heart racing and electricity
flowing throughout my body making my skin
produce goose bumps and tingling in my spine.

Before my mouth was dry
as if I was breathing in sand and
dying of dehydration but now...
Life.

Such power came to me and in the simplest
yet most powerful form.
There was no bolt of lightning that came
from Heaven and gave me strength.
There was no second wind
that came from some iron will to win.

This can only be defined as raw power.
It's not divine or unholy. It's not even...
Supernatural.
We all have this power.

When it hits us, all knowledge becomes oblivion.
Worries and fears disappear as the complex becomes clear.
In moments of passion, it over flows us all with emotion
and makes our eyes break out in tears.

This is the kiss. This is the power.
Damn those who abuse it.

Needs and Wants

We need to know the truth,
but we want to be entertained.
We need to know what's out there,
but we want to stay in this bubble.

We need to know who's watching us,
but I want to be the one watching others.
We need to start living our own lives, but
can't stop wanting to watch others live theirs.

We need to know who are enemies are,
but instead we want to know who the celebrities are.
We need to know where our future is,
but we want to know more about today.

Because we are watching what we want,
we are becoming blind to what we need.
Who am I to be saying this?
I'm someone who wants to know what we need.

Ted Buddy

I was taken against my will
and forced to spread my legs
and hear the awful satisfaction
as he screams in sinful delight
and tears my insides with his penis.

Makes noises like a rabid dog.
Howling and growling with sickly satisfaction
as he violates my body in the worst way.
I know now that Lucifer exists
because I've met his finest creation.

I was screaming for my mommy
and begging for this monster to stop.
But all that did was encourage him to do more.
So, he punched my mouth and broke my jaw.
I was no longer able to speak.
I had lost virtually all of my sanity
as he poured his vile fluids inside me.
I looked up in the sky
with salty bloody black eyes
and began to realize.

No longer will I dream of losing my virginity to my love
because he spread his poison inside me.
I will never get married because he will kill me
because I saw his face, and I can't defend myself.
My body and soul were beaten and broken
like a snail's shell after meeting a human foot.

The last image I saw
wasn't my children or my children's children.
Instead, I saw a huge rock, as I tried to
scream mixed with blood,
to scream through broken teeth
and bleeding gums.

Splash!
The earth was mixed with my blood and brains.
I can only thank God I left after the first blow
as he keeps doing it over and over again
until my face looks like a broken mirror.

I was a person with a dream.
I was going to college to be a teacher.
I was only 17 and loved to help people.
I was a virgin and that's all he saw,
and he used my good nature against me.

His name will survive long after he's gone
in textbooks, biographies, documentaries and movies.
But I will just get a column in the paper when they find me,
and, in time, my name will be forgotten.
You will remember the killer.
But how will you remember the victim?

What makes the killer's name more important?
What about our names?

A Character in Love

I see how she cries tonight,
wondering when the day she falls in love
will come and make her life better
by filling it with happiness and worth.

How I'd love to be the one to give her what she wants,
but there is one problem --
I don't exist.
I am only alive in the pages she reads.

She does not know how much it brings me joy
to give her what she needs
by fulfilling her desire to see her ideal mate
perform in my epic trials and labors --
to be the kind of man she would like to have.

I can remember the first night we met,
late one night after her first day at the library.
It was my first appearance
where I traveled through the underworld
to save my love.

How she sobbed as I was being cut by the demons,

and how she held herself as my skin was being
burned by the fires of the inner circles.
My heroic deeds put a smile on her face,
and seeing her smile gives me the greatest pleasure.
I only wish I could give her more.

Years go by, but still she sees me and adores
with each turn of the page.
No matter how many times she rereads my tales,
I try to deliver the same impact as if it
was the first time all over again.
There is nothing more precious to me
than seeing that wonderful smile
on this woman and to see her eyes upon me
making my pulse race and adrenaline flow
like a rapid river.

But alas, my love, showing her what some men can be
is also blinding her from what some men are.
How they are worse than the demons I slay
and scorch worse than the fires I go through.
How I wish I could stand by your side
and dispatch them like I would any villain
because of my love for this special woman.

But again,
I don't exist.
I can't be there for her.
I can never to be real.

For this harm I cause, I will never forgive myself,
    but I pray she doesn't lose faith.
    One day she will meet someone
    who excites her as I once did.

    He may not slay dragons,
    he may not battle demons,
    he may not be as good looking,
but he will have one thing in common with me.

    He will have her in his life,
    and he will love her for it.

Am I Crazy?

Am I crazy?
I am asked this every week
By the women in the bar or by
someone I meet any random day.
I am a lot of things that many aren't.

I'm sorry when it is
my fault.
For whatever wrong I've done,
I have the fortune and dignity to be a man
and admit responsibility and do what I can
to undo what has been done.

I'm humble.
I don't get on a high horse and speak
as if I'm the center of the universe
because I have thousands of friends online
or because I make millions of dollars.

I'm not blind.
 I choose to see the world in my own image,
and I have the courage to resist how others
would want it to be seen.
 Too many Fathers, Mothers, Sisters, Brothers,
Cousins, Nephews, and Nieces
have died for me to have this privilege.
It's a dishonor to them to ignore it.

I'm not a loner.
I just choose to listen to both sides
of an argument and make a decision
based on my own thinking and logic,
not just because I am a member of a party
or belong to a specific faction.

I'm not a saint.
I don't do what's right because of a code of
ethics or because the law tells me to do so.
I do what I feel is right because I listen
to the most important part of my body.
Yes, sometimes it may be seen
as the wrong thing, and, again,
I'm sorry, but if that's what I believe
needs to be done, It's going to get done.

Am I crazy because I choose
to see things in ways nobody cares to look or
because I think with an open mind and do things
because I feel that is the appropriate action to take?
Probably. But at least I don't hide it because there's one thing
I can say that I know I am that sums it all up.

I'm Real.

A Father's Thoughts at his Daughter's Wedding

I have to say how nice it is
to finally get the chance to speak here.
> (After all I am the one who paid
> for the whole damn thing).

After looking at this family that is about
to join with mine, I'm so happy.
> (I'd be happier behind a gun turret
> with all of you in front of it).

I hope that you are all very happy
to become part of my family.
> (After looking at all you, I'm sure
> you're tired of the constant inbreeding).

I know my daughter picked a fine man.
> (I guess the bum on the street corner said no.
> At least, I could tell he was human).

He is, without a doubt, the luckiest man
in the entire world.

(That my daughter has the lowest standards possible,
and she is probably going blind and senile).

When I first heard the news about this wedding,
I was hysterical.
(Mostly because I thought it was a joke
until I saw the ring, and then I started rewriting my will).

And now that I see these two together,
I am relieved.
(Because I know now that there is a hell,
and I'm going to start going to church).

So now I will end this
with a toast.
(To the open bar because these screwdrivers
are the only reason I can stand this pack of mutants).

Congratulations to the bride and groom.
May their love last forever.

Really?!

Do you have to really go there?
Do you think you have to act
like a complete idiot to get your way?
Why can't you just say you didn't know
and you're sorry?
Is it really so wrong for someone to admit fault?

"Nobody ever told me!"

Nobody has to tell you a damn thing!
We live in a world where you can find
the information through hundreds of
outputs, and you're telling me you can't
take five minutes to find it out for yourself?
Don't bother me with your snob-like attitude
because you think you're too good to do stuff yourself.

"Everyone else is doing it."

Seriously, when we were kids, didn't our parents
talk to us about jumping off a bridge?
You're going to throw that excuse at me
like it makes it any better?
Why don't you just say,
"We were following orders"
while you're at it?
Because just like the previous excuse,
it's hollow in reasoning and pathetic.

"Life owes me."

Life owes a lot of people that are probably
living far worse lives than us.
But we do not because we owe but
because it's what we're suppose to do.
We're supposed to go to school.
We're supposed to stay out of jail.
We're supposed to take care of ourselves.
We're supposed to take care of others.

If you're not doing your part then how do
you expect to get out of life
what you didn't put into it?
Nothing is just giving no matter what class
you're in, it must be taken.

Really,
since when did it become ok for adults
to make children seem more civilized?
We are suppose to be setting the example,
not lowering it.

I say this not to provoke
but to invoke.
Grow up.

Music Television

I remember when I was young.
There was a pioneer giving us
something the people had never
seen before:

Music videos.

Getting to see my favorite artist
perform their favorite songs and
actually seeing the story
behind the words.

It was awesome being a kid
and having something to turn to
when we were up late at night
and there was nothing to watch.
So, we turned on that channel and jammed
to hours of random videos but all good.

I remember how I would rush home right after school
just to catch the *Total Request Live*
and see who was the celebrity to show up.
All my votes never made it to number one.

I guess I had bad taste in music.

I just have one question.
Why is now showing what it is called?
Now all it seems to show is shows
based on "Reality," shows about people being idiots
and movies that only appeal to bigger idiots.
Where are the music videos?

Perhaps, I am too old to understand,
or maybe I'm just confused by the name.
Maybe it should be called Mainstream television
or something else that starts with "M."

I don't know the answer but I only know one thing.
I miss my music videos.

The Ultimate Question

Wars have been started over it,
and more blood has been spilt
over one simply question.
What will happen when we die?

Is there such a place as Heaven?
Can there be a place better than Earth?
If there is, I'd give my life to be there.
But ending my life would only lead to damnation.

And if there is a Heaven, what of Hell?
To think that there is a place
that can be worse than where we are now is
a thought so terrible I don't even want to ponder.

But even worse, what if there is nothing
on the other side?

What if it's just oblivion?
We live this life and that's it.
Could we really accept that?
Think of what that means.

That means that the billions of people
have been killed for their dedication.
If there is nothing on the other side, then
every death over religion was in vain.
The lives that could've been spared
but instead were condemned.
Such a terrible thought.

As I wonder this, I ask myself the ultimate question.
Do I want to know the truth?
I honestly don't think I could handle such answer.
So, how do I move on from my curiosity?
I will just live as I've always lived,
thinking every day is my last.

I will move on, wish for Heaven,
and pray for those in Hell.
But if there is indeed nothing
and this is all there is...

Well then there really isn't anything
to say, is there?

Payback

You think you're so smart and slick.
You lied to get where you are.
You've stepped on people weaker
and stolen their ideas.

I was one of them.
I saw how you used your charm
and your wits to get places.
But now it's time for payback,
and payback's a bitch.

Your ego is so big
it blinds you from seeing other things,
like the fact that for 6 months
I have been sleeping with your wife.

What's sad is she comes to me.
And I mean that in more ways than one.

So, while you go on with your promotion,
I leave this letter on your desk.
Just so you know, your wife told me
your child is actually mine.

Death House

Damn this destination of death
where we go to lose our creativity
and the uniqueness of the human spirit,
to convert to the will of corporations and society.

Where our minds were once free of limitations,
are now bound by the invisible rules of society.
Stealing from them the best years of their lives
by teaching them how to survive in "the real world."

They destroy our care-free environment
to place us in place in a world created by Darwin
where we go from playing in our imaginations
to taking tests on desks in classrooms.

Why couldn't I have read Wordsworth earlier?
The way he spoke of us until
we came here, to this place of corruption,
the first stage of our childhood robbery.

They have us wake up earlier than we should
and place us in cold classrooms with crappy chairs;
my back still aches because I couldn't fit in those seats,
and for that I will always hate them.

Lunches were always the best time before I went
to these death houses.
I remember how I would get grilled cheese sandwiches
and Dominos Pizza with those tasty bread sticks.

They feed us meatless meatloaf
and have us drink milk that could be
mistaken for vanilla pudding,
and they call it healthy.
I'd rather eat my own boogers
and drink my own bile.
It would taste the same
but at least look better.
To hell with the enforcers of "Society"
turning the dreamers to conformers.
They erase our fantasies for logic
and say that you're taking our heads out of the clouds.

More like they're digging into our chest,
breaking our chest bone wide open.
And after digging through our blood, veins and organs,
they rip out our pumping bright red hearts.

Could they have at least worn gloves?
That way I don't feel your dry, greasy fingers
and use the dirt under their fingernails
to poison our hearts and turn them black.

The only lesson I've ever learned from these locations of
education
is that the world's a cruel place, and we've lost our paradise.
Lesson is well learned,
their mission accomplished.

Super Sexuality

WOW!
Have you snap, crackled, and popped?
Who are you to be talking about my sexuality
just because I have a colorful costume

and I walk around with blue tights, a red cape,
and a red letter on my chest?
Why are you always on my case
and thinking you're better than me?

Excuse me for not wearing a morbid animal instead
because it's not my fault your life is crap.

Nan Nan Nan, Nan
Nan Nan, Nan Nan Nan.

That's all I hear from you, and
you think I have it so good
just because I'm labeled the man of steel,
and I can't say ouch?

Your only weakness is being human.
How do you think I feel that I can lift a mountain
and survive a nuclear blast from ground zero,
yet be stopped by a little green rock the size of a thimble.
Yeah, I feel very manly about that.

Slap!
That's what you deserve --

always whining because your parents were murdered.
My parents sent me away to live at a farm
and practically wrote me a card saying "best of luck."

You had a butler to replace your father.
I had a talking crystal. What the hell?
You know why I have so much power?
Because I could never afford to buy all
that junk you have hidden away in that cave.

Speaking of everything –
why do you get on my case for all the powers?
How do you fit everything into your utility belt?
No matter the situation, there's something in that belt
that magically fits in that little pocket and saves your butt.

You get on my case because I can't feel a simple bomb's boom.
Well, I think you and I have something in common there.
Because you've been spending too much time in a cave,
I wonder if you can even get some boom.

But then again,
I guess that's the real reason
you have your "boy" wonder.
I don't need x-ray to see through that.

DAMN!
I guess for him its wham bam
thank you, Batman.
That boy is more colorful than me.

POW!

That look you have on your face shows
exactly how I feel about your question.
Just because I don't go around dressed like a bad ass,
and I have a reputation of being a big blue boy scout,
doesn't make me any less of a man.

So, you go on and fight crime the way you want to.
But next time, keep your comments to yourself.
AH! That's Lois screaming.
It's time for me to find a phone booth
and dress because if I'm going to save her,
I've got to look Fabulous!
Snap Snap.

Just kidding,
you homophobe.

Dark Skies

I'm writing here in the dark,
can't see where I'm writing.
I pray my words reach this paper
for they will be my last.

The power is gone
and the batteries are low.
We can't get a signal out,
so nobody is coming for help.

I can't hear the screams of my sister,
I have gone deaf
due to the loud beatings of my heart,
to the horrible sounds from outside the house.

Thunder
like being at ground zero of a nuclear blast.
The clashing of objects I can't see,
smashing against the shields on my windows
and, of course,
the annoying alarm of a cheap Honda Civic.

Then it happens!
My parents heard the sound of glass break.
Something was banging against mom and dad's bedroom
wall.
So, dad shoved us into my closet,
and mom told us to shut up.

Five minutes pass, and my sister can't stop crying.
I tell her that we're going to be alright.
She hugs me like I was her teddy bear.
But then we heard it.

Boom!
Something had gone through our parent's bedroom wall.
We can't hear mom or dad anywhere.
Don't they know our line of defense is breached?

I ran out to look and left my sister behind.
I ran into mom and dad's bedroom.
I ran like a cheetah.
I ran, and I saw.

I saw the hole in the wall.
I saw the Honda Civic used to make that hole.
I saw my parents underneath that Honda Civic.
I saw the roof shaking, and I knew.

I knew that it wasn't going to hold.

So, I went back to my sister
and started writing these words.

I want people to know.
I want them to know what happened here.
So, they know what I experienced the day we died --
a death that shouldn't be wished on anybody.

It's happened.
The roof has given way.
We can see that spinning elevator
that's going to take us to those dark skies.
I will put this letter in my pocket
and pray for my body to be found.

To the person that finds this letter,
Thank you.

To my friends and relatives who survived,
Good Bye.

Bada Bing John

This is a story about John.
Oh, Johnny boy --
how he shines
when he plays the trickster
with his confidence and wit.

Playing tricks on all of us
by getting us when we least expect it.
When he walked into the room,
he loved nothing more than to
hear angels sing and the lights
to point all at him when a prank occurred.

But he also let known his weakness,
and that's what we used against him.
He prided himself a ladies man.
John would always talk about
how his great white shark
can make blue-backs look like trout.

How he would dazzle us
with his stories of stupid
girls who fell for his 1980s
pickup lines and false ego.
Those girls weren't stupid.
They were probably in the mood
for a good laugh.

He claimed that women

should be honored to be in his league
which to everybody else
was the league beneath
everybody else.

Then he said that we should all aspire
to be like him.
Now that was sugar.
That made me diabetic.

So, we all invited him to a strip club
and got him a lap dance from the most
popular stripper in South Beach.
Oh, how glorious it was to see.

How that stripper rubbed her breasts
in his face and grinded up and down his body.
He had the biggest smile on his face
when I told her to show him the goods.

When she dropped her thong
and revealed a surprise package,
the look on his face was priceless.
Bada Bing John.

Suicide

I'm enjoying this so much -- the fact that I've reclaimed some sense of honor after what this man did, like slipping into a warm bath after a long hot day of labor only the water in the tub is blood. I never realized what freedom is until I crossed the ultimate boundary. Because I lay here next to somebody who had wronged me and is now dead. Stolen from me that which I hold dear. That I would die for to regain but it's something that can't be given back. It's gone forever. I tracked him down like a dog, and then with this hatchet, I carved him like a Thanksgiving turkey. Now, I'm drenched with his blood. I honestly don't know what is better -- the warm blood dripping down my face or the fact that vengeance is mine. I honestly can't tell which is better. I see a puddle of blood near his body. I think I'll

splash some more on my body to stay warm.
Oh my god in heaven. Why can't I see my
reflection?

As I lay here

I lay here on my death bed, and yet I rejoice.
I reflect on my life and start to smile
on what I have done and what I'm going to reclaim
as I go on to a better place.

I see my family now crying over me, wishing I wasn't going.
How I wish I had the strength to say don't.
Socrates said, "Death is the greatest blessing a mortal has."
I go to now back to the woman I love more than life itself.

I go to see my love,
the one that made me truly live.
The way she kissed me, sending chills down my spine
and making her stand on her toes as I run my hand
through her hair which is as soft as her lips.

Being without her was hell, and now I will go to her in heaven.
I imagine us meeting again at our beach house
where we made love and got away from the world.
How I want to feel our feet together as we rub them
in the sand and wait for the water to come in and wash the sand off
our feet as we both breathe in the sweet ocean breeze
while enjoying a sunset fit for a romantic novel.

I will relive the moments when I bounced my daughter on my knee
and played football with my son, watching them grow.
Only difference is I will control time and make sure they grow

just a little bit more slowly than normal, so I can enjoy being a dad more.

I don't fear death because, truth be told, I longed for it.
I have lost so many of my loved ones, and now I go to see them again.
My family will miss me, as I missed my loved ones but they will see me again. Until that time comes,
I love them all and goodbye.

Sad Profession

My face is red.
My bruises are blue.
You're going to wish you were dead
because I'm going to sue you.

My lawyer is on my speed dial
and he's won 13 straight.
I haven't been to court in a while
but now I've got a date.

Thank you for being the newest defendant
because my bank account is a little dry.
But now I'll be getting your money,
so, please, feel free to cry.

I love getting hurt at a store
because they pay me to stay silent.

Space

I can fill the pages of this poem
by filling it with words to burn the heart
and warm the blood to the point it boils
and creates a rush of passion.

I can place objects of worth around my home
and make this a home fit for a king
that would welcome a wonderful princess
to turn into my queen.

I can fill your head with dreams
of the life we can have together as man and wife.
As we journey the world and see it's wonders,
I would be the spouse of its greatest treasure.

But the one object I can't seem to fill
is the heart that beats inside your chest,
no matter how much I put into poems
or how attractive I made my lifestyle.

There is something there that just blocks us
and tells us just one simple fact.
The dream of you and I is only that --
a dream.

So, now I'm here alone
and resting here next to the most important space
a person should be concerned with --
the other side of my bed.

Get Up!

One door opens...that's what they say.
But what's a door to someone who won't walk through it?
There's plenty of fish...that's nice but one problem --
some people have no patience and get motion sickness.

Left, right, upward, and downward, and, if you don't
position yourself,
you get sprayed in the face and look stupid and sad.
With a risk like that, some would just chicken out
and pay 50 for an hour.

It isn't over until the fat lady sings...the fat lady needs to
shut the hell up.
Her singing sucks, and it's a weak metaphor
for someone who is losing and wants to give up anyway.
Why does the lady singing always have to be fat?
Stereotypical pricks.

Why do we use these to pick people up?
Why can't we say what they need to hear?
Because it is the only way to wipe away the dirt
covering their pride and esteem.

"I lost my job."
So, get up and take a shower!
Dust yourself off and find something.

If I can juggle 2, you can find 1.

"My girlfriend left me."
So, get up and take a shower!
Go to places and meet with other singles
who are just like you.

"My life is over!"
So, get up and take a shower!

There are people living their lives
in the worst ways.

In hospitals, wheelchairs, beds with no mattresses, in caves,
one room apartments, or under bridges, lonely, starving,
with no one to turn to, being poor in every way.
Do you have a bathroom?
Do you have hot water?
You know what to do.

A Brilliant Robin

Ever since you and Mindy met,
I have never been able to keep my eyes off you.
When I saw you sail in with Olive
and flex your big forearms,
I knew you were a brilliant Robin.

I never needed toys
cause I watch you for amusement.
I never had to go fishing with grandpa
because I was watching a king on the screen.

The way you made us laugh with Comic Relief.
It was like watching poetry in motion,
like you were the leader of a dead society.
And you touched our hearts with more than comedy.

You've been everywhere from cold Moscow
to seeing a good morning in Vietnam.
Just to see you do what you can do
is a real awakening.

The way you can change colors
by turning into a big blue clown,
making dreams of a pauper come true.
You became the best friend anyone knew.

You've even changed sexes,
and proved that being an old lady
can be funny and lovable.
It's almost like you have artificial intelligence.

Then, there is your voice
that hides so many others.
If I didn't know any better Jack,
I'd say you were a machine covered in furry skin.

You can't be real.
It's like you popped out of Neverland
because you never get old in spirit.
There's always a fresh joke for you to tell.

No birdcage can hold you.
I would have an easier time
trying to catch air with hands.
Your humor is what dreams can come.

You have done so much a man can do.
It's almost like you have Insomnia
because you never seem to sleep.
You should be man of the year.

If there was a museum of you,
I'd wait all night there with happy feet.
I'd take a picture of you,
and rush it to one hour photo.

I hope somehow I get to meet you someday.

So, until then I will say thank you for everything.
You are a brilliant Robin, and, until there is another,
Good Hunting Mr. Williams.

The Right Words

You are so special to me.
You are beautiful and kind.
You can make a blind man see.
I'd give my all to make you mine.

It's difficult to make this dream a reality.
You're like an angel from the sky.
I am unworthy to the many.
That is what makes me cry.

I don't know what to do or say.
I want to say something new,
something that hasn't been said to this day.
These words are powerful and few.

If spending an eternity with you would cost a lifetime
of pain and misery,
I'd do it
in a heartbeat times two.

These seem to be the right words to say.
All I have to say now is this:
I love you
and Happy Valentine's Day.

The Past Returns

Seventy years ago there was an attack on an island,
another attack again on land,
with more death and dark clouds
blinding all the eyes and silencing the tongues.

Once a horrible genocide
almost wiped out the oldest religion,
and we closed our eyes to it
because we weren't provoked.

Now we see another genocide,
and, again, we close our eyes to it,
but there's no religion involved.
It's just people, so that makes it okay.

Once there was a battle in the jungle,
and some didn't understand why we were there.
Now, there is a war in a dry desert,
and the same confusion is back.

Time and time again,
I see these men in their sheets.
Carrying on a tradition long thought dead
but still keep the war alive in their black hearts.

For 30 years we were focused
on a clock of doomsday.
Now, with more atomic enemies than one,
it only seems like a matter of time.

Is it just me or is there
just a strange pattern?
I can't believe I'm scared of
what past will return next.

One Question

There are a lot of questions one would ask God.
Some would seem normal, and the rest would be odd.
Why are we here, and where do we go when we die,
and do our lives flash at the blink of an eye?

What was the point of our life?
Why did we have to go through strife?
Why couldn't we be rich?
Why was my wife such a bitch?

My question would be in the odd.
I bet when I ask, God will nod.
I know he'll be annoyed as a matter of fact
when I ask why do we have hair on our butt and back?

What's the reasoning for something like that?
To have hair where we can't shave seems a bit whack.
When I would go camping I never went without a shirt,
and, if I did, you would hear a gun, and I would get hurt.

I ask this because it concerns me personally
because of the reason I'm here -- somebody confused me for
Yogi.

Happy Holidays

4:00 a.m. open with special sales.
4:00 a.m. wake crazy consumers.
They wait in line giving no room for cuts,
yet they're ready to cut throats to get in front of the others.

The doors open, and people stampede
over cigarette butts and peoples' necks.
Because shoes are 75% off,
a woman now lies dead by a new pair.

A bottle of perfume is only $50.
A woman takes a spray on the wrist to give it a try
then takes a shot in the eyes by another woman.
Now, that bottle is gone and she's left dry.

Kids are grabbing used games the game shops,
but what are they doing up at 4 in the morning?
Why are their parents letting them play games filled with
blood?
God forbid they fought over a book by Lord Byron.

Then there are the little 13 year old girls
walking around the lingerie section meant for women.
Only, I don't think they're shopping for their mothers.
Are they looking for something to wear at the beach?

Old hags even come and spread their dust.
It must be the one time of year I see new
life in them as they haul ass. Makes me wonder

what happened to "What would Jesus do?"

Finally, there are all the juvenile wannabes
walking around like they are so bad
with their pants blow their waste.
I hope they like it later when their butts
are touched by Bubba's special candy cane.

I feel sorry for the employees who have no choice,
as the customers yell and curse at them like slave masters.
For making them be there, they should be the ones
yelling at the customers saying, "Go to hell you stingy bastards!"

Brand new sales happen here
and there as the day goes by.
More and more bones are broken
while people on stretchers pray not to die.

People are running either to sales or to get out of the way.
What a great time and day to go to the mall
when people of all ages are spreading the holiday spirit
with fights, lacerations, and handcuffs for all.

Next time just go to the discount stores where
they have the same prices all year round.
It's better than your kids coming to see you on Christmas
when you're buried 6 feet under the ground.

A False Survivor Story

As I lay here in the E.R.,
I think over my story of how I survived
falling from the sky in a plane after it
is struck by lightning and landing in the Atlantic.

I am going to say this –
I went to the bathroom after
just proposing to my girlfriend --
or I should say now ex-girlfriend,
may she rest in peace.

We were together for years,
and things were going well until
she started feeling weird, so I felt
she wanted to move to the next step.

So, I planned a weekend in Paris
where a hotel would be ready to welcome
a soon to be newlywed couple
to enjoy their bliss.

While I was in the back of the plane,
I heard an explosion as if a stick of T.N.T went off in front of me,
and the plane started going down along with my heart.
I was sent airborne and hit my head on the smoke alarm

while going deaf to the sounds of the people screaming.

I felt like being caught in a spider web.
Because of the force, I couldn't move anything.
But as soon as the adrenaline kicked in,
I started moving out to get to my girlfriend.
Sorry, late-girlfriend.

As I got out and looked at the passengers, I saw the terror --
the terror of certain death, and I saw her.
She looked at me with tears in her eyes,
and reached out for me to come with her.
I will say how I tried with all my strength
to get to her, but, as the plane went faster,
I was pushed back near the bathroom.
I shouted out that I love her and I will see her soon,
and I braced for the impact. Then, I blacked out.

This is what I will tell the reporters -- this story --
and deny them the truth.
That after the plane was falling and
after I got out of the bathroom, I saw her.

She reached out for me and said I love you.
I looked back at her and said,
"I would've believed you if you had said 'Yes."
Then I ran back into the bathroom
and hoped that I'd survive the crash.

I will carry this with me the rest of my life,
but at least I will be alive and at least
I have my best friend Jeremy.

Sorry, soon to be ex-best friend.

What a sign!

It's so
amazing
how one
finger is
capable
of meaning
a lot. Its
meaning
can be a good
or bad. What
could have been going on inside the head of one man that gave him the idea to give such a small gesture a really big meaning? What an easy way of just telling someone that you either don't like them or you want to do something to them. It's so strange how a meaning can be fit to one small finger. Like the mystical bond between the driver and the car, it just fits I wonder how it would be fitting if it were a different finger. It couldn't be the pinky because that would seem more of a joke than an actual insult. What if it was the ring finger? If somebody had an expensive ring, that might give some insight into how much the person giving the finger actually means it. It definitely couldn't be the index or the thumb. They're already important enough as is. So it's only appropriate that such a saying belongs to this middle finger. Hell, without it, we pretty much would just have to cut it off. It's so strange how it all fits to this finger. What a great sign.

Your Sanity, Your Handicap

Yes,
I think things you people are scared to think.
My mind goes places you're too scared to be.
I can tolerate hideous sites
and stomach grotesque images.

But I can also accept certain truths
that make you uncomfortable to talk about.
I say things that will cross your lines.
I do things that will make a situation awkward.

I talk to certain people you don't want to be around,
and I'm friends with people not even I can understand.
I have religious texts, and yet I don't practice.
I go to events that don't even concern me
and listen to music that is in languages
I can't speak.

You say I need help, that I have lost my sanity.
You mean I'm not supposed to act freely
just because you're too scared to do the same?
That I'm suppose to follow in line and support
your conformist insecurities?
Um...go to hell.

What you would consider my handicap,
I consider to be my advantage over you.
You live in a circle of normality --
every day the same routines, boring hobbies,
a moment of intimacy here and there.
Round and round you go on the same
boring pattern.

I'm too big for your box,
and you can't survive in my circle.
You think me insane. Well, then I guess I am.
Thank god for the gift you can't handle.

What I Wish I Could Say

If you agree with someone just because it sounds patriotic
or because it's what the rest of the party is doing
and you don't really have an opinion,
you're not being a patriot -- you're just being an idiot.

If you're the loudest person in the church
because you think that makes you seem
the most devoted, it doesn't.
It just makes you the loudest person in the room.
Now, lower the volume before I sue you for
making me deaf.

To all the parents who defend their kids
even when they are in the wrong
and blame the adults --
you're not being a good parent!
Start giving your kids what they need
or get rid of them.

To all the people who are so shocked
when a scandal happens and a "role model"
shatters the ideals he built his empire on --
honestly when power gets to our heads,

how do you not expect us to go out of line?

To all the women that say,
"Just because I dress slutty, doesn't mean I am slutty."--
That's fine, just don't get mad at me when
I dress like I have money and
then get pissed after waking up with me
in my one room studio.

And to all the guys...don't act like I'm leaving you alone.
Stop working extra hard at the gym when a woman
is working out right next to you.
The only thing she's really noticing
is that you're about to have heart attack.

Everyday there's something we'd like to say
but don't because we don't want to offend.
Well, nobody ever worried about offending me
when I was young and fat.

So, I feel no obligation
to keep my mouth shut.

Show me Love

You give us shows about
"True Love"
by giving a guy and girl
a few weeks to choose
who they'd love to make out with.

That is not love.
Love doesn't take a few weeks to work
unless it's something you read or
watch in a movie.

Then you show me
the lives of celebrities.
Their marriages don't last
as is, but when they get on television,
the process just speeds up.

You want to give me a show on
"True Love,"
here's how you do it.
Give me a reality show about two people
who get on each other's nerves
every moment of the day.

Getting into arguments about work, about the house,
about life in general.

Have them ready to go nuts. If, at that point, they still go to bed together, and they still kiss each other goodnight, then that's a show I would love to see on the air.

Loyalty

Trust.
It's the most crucial decision we make
in life.

Who should be picked to run this country?
Who do I believe can enforce the laws?
Who do can I spend the rest of my life with?
Who do I trust to take care of me?

Where can I go for my education?
Where can I find a good hospital for my pregnant wife?
Where can I raise my kids in peace?
Where can I settle down?
Where is my money safe?

So many decisions
that seem like forks in the road,
leading to any number of outcomes.
We make these decisions on leaps of faith.
But what happens when that faith is
betrayed?

Jobs are disappearing.
Dreams are shattered
like pieces of a broken mirror.

Money is lost,
becoming transparent.
People are becoming desperate,
taking entry level jobs.
And these people are in their 40s.

Children are neglected.
Bullying is on the rise
for whatever reason,
and education is becoming a joke.
Teachers are fighting a losing battle.

Politicians.
Left, Right, Undecided.
There are so many sides, and the
biggest problem is that nothing is getting done.
Every side wants their way.
Every side is willing to take forever to win.
No side is giving in,
and that is why we're suffering.

How do you expect people to stay loyal,
when everything they believe in
is falling to rubble?
Degrees are in the streets
and dreams are forever shattered.
How do you recover from betrayal?

Trust me when I say,
It's a long road ahead.

Nice Guys Finish Best

Who was it that said,
"Nice guys finished last?"
Was it a philosopher or a doctor
who made that claim off years of study
and research?

Or was it some douche that
had nothing better to do than sit around
and not make a thing of himself
and spend so much time in regret that
he would make one claim make his life have meaning?

Who turned life into a race?
I haven't lived a fast life, and here's why.
I wasn't the bad boy in high school who
got in trouble with the police, but
I also wasn't the nerd who didn't go out
and studied every minute of the day.

I was just a guy who did what felt right
whether it was studying for a test
or going out to spend time
with the people that made my life great.

I am not a millionaire like so many others
that have taken the fast route.
Some went down the path of drugs,
others the path of sports and entertainment,
and some just became thieves in the political or financial ring.
They all started getting what they wanted quick --

the money, cars, house, company.
But then came all the stuff that took up their time:
promotions, shoots, and meetings.
Twenty-two-hour days that go by so fast
it only feels like an eight-hour shift.
The price for being a millionaire.

I took the slow route --a job that may not make me rich
but
will give me the time I need with my family.
I may not have the fancy cars or the big house but
there are some things I have that make me
better than any millionaire out there.

I have my privacy because nobody wants to hear
from someone who isn't on the top of the mountain.
I have children whom I can recall their birthday, know their favorite color,
go to all of their soccer and baseball games, and go to their school plays.

People know the shape of my heart
when I have time to donate the little money I have
and spend time with the ones who lost their way
and spun off the track.

Unlike the millionaire who gives just for
"Good publicity,"
who throws money at the problems
thinking that's all that's needed to solve it.

I have a wife who also has a good job
and does her part by the kids.
She knows me and knows she's my reason for living.
My muse, my love.

Unlike the millionaires wife.
She sits around and watches "reality" tv
or some cooking show, like she could cook anyway.
She is probably some teen out of high school that's
obviously
digging for gold and waiting for her husband to die.
When that happens, she won't be there for him,
and that's when he'll realize his mistakes and cry.

When it's my time, my family will rejoice,
and I will be thankful for all that I've experienced
because, unlike some, I may have finished last,
but that just means I had more time
before I reached that line.

Life may be a race, but that doesn't mean the fastest ones win.
Remember the hare lost the race for a reason.
We only get one chance at life.
It's a shame to go so fast that you don't know where you've been.

Personal Belief

If you can't be yourself around strangers -- what chance do you possibly have at Life?

Thank you for your support and I hope you've enjoyed my work. Until the next is written...

Sincerely

Anthony Labson

www.ingramcontent.com/pod-product-compliance
Lightning Source LLC
Chambersburg PA
CBHW071757200526
45167CB00017B/381